FACE *to* FACE

GABRIELLE WARNOCK

JEFF O'CONNELL

Published by Trident Press Ltd
Editor: Paula Vine
Design: Jane Stark

Text: © Foreword: Fintan O'Toole
       © In Search of a Book: Jeff O'Connell
       © Biographies: Gabrielle Warnock

Layout and design: © Trident Press Ltd

Photographs:©   ABC Studio: 112, 154
                Connacht Tribune: 59
                Bill Doyle: 8
                Irish Times: 34
                Tadhg Keady: 120, 210
                Jimmy Walshe: 121
                Yann Studio: 57, 62, 133, 152, 171, 199
                All other photographs by Monica Rigney
                Cover illustration by Jimmy Lawlor

British Library Cataloguing in Publication Data
A CIP catalogue record for this book is available from the British Library

ISBN 1 900724 46 4

Printed in European Union

Trident Press Ltd., Empire House,175 Piccadilly, Mayfair, London, W1V 9DB
Tel: 0207 491 8770; Fax: 0207 491 8664; e-mail: admin@tridentpress.ie
Station House, Clifden, Co. Galway Tel: 095 22024; Fax: 095 22068
Internet: www.tridentpress.com

CONTENTS

*A*s you work your way through a contemporary best-selling novel like, for example, Tom Wolfe's *A Man in Full*, your eye is drawn again and again to the photograph of the author on the inside back cover. The picture is part of the package. There he is in a full page colour portrait, an elegant black-brimmed white hat on his head, a white suit with black-bordered white handkerchief popping up from the breast pocket, and the knot of his black tie with white polka dots finishing off the perfectly co-ordinated effect. The face is tanned and handsome, with a wicked glint in the dark eyes and a superior smirk playing about the lips. The chosen pose is that of a cool, dandified Southern gentleman whose seen it all and remained coolly unimpressed.

This picture is not just an appendage to the novel, but an integral part of it. It is there to tell us how to read the book, to signal the detached, world-weary tone of voice in which we are meant to say the words inside our heads as we scan them on the page. Like a face on a totem pole, it is there to scare off awkward questions about the author's intentions or the limits of his world-view. In that sense, it is an emblem of much of what is wrong with the marriage of writing and PR, of author and image, in contemporary publishing. Too often, between the reader and the writer come a series of more or less blatant advertisements, in which the personality of the writer comes first and the quality of the book straggles along in second place.

These days authors, and to some extent other artists, are expected to be the principal salesmen for their own work. They have to give interviews, appear on television, embark on elaborate reading tours, do signings and personal appearances, and, above all, be photographed for the inside back covers looking as moody and mysterious, as enigmatic and sexy, as their bedraggled features will allow.

Nor are these demands placed merely on the living artist, for this is an age when the faces of dead writers and painters have become as central to the tourist industry as the

Eiffel Tower, the Taj Mahal or the Cliffs of Moher. In Ireland, Yeats, Joyce, Kavanagh, Behan, even Beckett look down from t-shirts, tea towels and the walls of pubs, as if their hard, serious words were dispensable and only the accidental arrangement of physical features with which they were born were really immortal. You don't have to read *Ulysses* in order to make James Joyce your own.

Not for nothing does a writer like John McGahern, whose picture graces this volume, sometimes suggest, half-joking and wholly in earnest, that he would love to have hired some suave, clean-cut handsome man to have been, for all public purposes, 'John McGahern'. This hired virtual author would do the book tours, answer the questions, sign the title pages, go to the awards ceremonies, and, above all, be pictured on the book, leaving the real author to get on with the quiet, lonely, essentially private business of writing. Art, after all, has, as Saul Bellow put it, 'something to do with the achievement of stillness in the midst of chaos . . . with an arrest of attention in the midst of distraction.' What is the author's own image if not another distraction?

Many great writers have extended such fantasies as McGahern's into their entire aesthetic. James Joyce, through the figure of Stephen Daedalus in *A Portrait of the Artist as a Young Man*, imagines the writer as an invisible, indifferent creature, off somewhere polishing his fingernails while the book he or she has created lives its own life. W.B Yeats reminds us that the man who sits down at the breakfast table is not at all the same person as the poet who takes up the pen to write. The writer, as Yeats would have it, assumes a mask, perhaps a different one for every work. And our business as readers is with the mask, not with the face behind it. Shakespeare's plays, for example, are none the worse, and perhaps even somewhat better, for the fact that we do not have a contemporary portrait of their author and have no real idea of what he looked like.

There is, though, another side to the story. Writing may be a lonely, essentially private act, but it has a public purpose. It is, in one form or another, an intervention in the world. To have stillness in the midst of chaos, in Bellow's formulation, you need the chaos as well as the stillness. If art is contrary, anti-clockwise, somehow outside or beyond the everyday, those very qualities depend on the immediate, contingent, mundane world of flesh and blood, of time and place. If some books become timeless and universal, they do so, paradoxically, because of the way they emerge from a very particular time and place. To pretend that they happen in a human and social vacuum is just as dishonest as the most cynical kind of image-making.

Even if artists wear masks, in other words, they are not faceless. Somewhere between the packaged images of the publishing and art industries on the one hand and the austere invisibility imagined by Stephen Daedalus on the other, there is a simpler, more truthful kind of authorial presence. The photographs collected here capture that presence beautifully.

It is important that these pictures come from the most natural and proper meeting place for writers and readers, a bookshop. Not, moreover, just another branch of some global bookselling empire, but the real, vibrant, vividly individual mecca for curious readers that is Kennys of Galway. Kennys, like any other shop, is a place where commodities are sold. But it is also a part of a much wider cultural community, where books are far more than commodities. Here, dead books come alive again as someone discovers a volume they didn't even know they were looking for. Here, the vital connection between writer and reader is made and re-made dozens of times a day.

The most important thing that these photographs remind us of is that writers are also readers. What binds together the otherwise diverse people whose faces you will find between these covers is not just the fact that they are distinguished writers, artists or intellectuals. It is the more haphazard, chaotic and apparently arbitrary fact that, at one time or another, each of them happened to wander into the same bookshop off a narrow street in a smallish city in the West of Ireland. And mostly they ended up there for exactly the same reason that everyone else does, to have a good root on the shelves and have their eye struck by some title on the spine of a book that connects with some memory, desire or curiosity within themselves.

Every writer, after all, is essentially a re-writer, a new filter for words, ideas, stories, images and metaphors that have been written, or at least imagined, before. Even if, to take two of the writers who show their faces here, Billy Roche had never read or seen a play by John Arden, he exists in a theatrical culture on which Arden has left an indelible imprint. Mary Robinson's public face bears some of the features of Noel Browne. Dermot Bolger has some of the blood of Liam O'Flaherty in his literary veins. David Malouf and Colm Tóibín connect across the continents. Nell McCafferty's journalism and Eavan Boland's poems inhabit, somehow, the same language. Paul Muldoon writes poetry in a world where the wry brilliance of Miroslav Holub has left its mark.

This, for writers and artists, is the most important sense in which they are public people. However lonely the act of writing or painting or thinking, it is also, in this sense, conducted in the midst of a crowd of living and dead presences. Together, these pictures form just such a crowd and animate, as they do so, the teemingly inhabited world in which every individual act of creation takes place.

Sadly, some of these images remind us, too, that art itself is a defiance of death, an attempt to outlast the inevitable end. As we look at them now, we see the dead: Michael Hartnett, Seán Keating, Allen Ginsberg, Gerald Hanley, George Campbell, Adele Dalsimer, Jim Kemmy, Mary Lavin, Seán Dunne, Miroslav Holub, Noel Browne, Tomás de Bhaldraithe, Eilís Dillon, Richard Ellman, Estyn Evans and many others, as they should be seen, among the living. The shelves of a good bookshop and the minds of thoughtful people are among the few places where the dead and the living exist without distinction, in the great democracy of words and images. In this sense, too, these pictures reflect a kind of truth. They bring to life that daydream in which many of us indulge from time to time when we imagine an ideal dinner party in which the guests can be summoned either from beyond the grave or just from down the road.

Informal, colloquial and unpretentious, these photographs occupy a calm resting place in the war between the demands of celebrity on the one hand and the desire to be invisible on the other, a sort of truce in the war between commercial packaging and artistic integrity. The subjects are respected but not revered, recognised but not intruded upon, marked out but not turned into icons. For readers and viewers, the photographs put flesh on the way we often feel when we're reading a book, or looking at a painting or listening to a courageous and intelligent politician. We imagine in these moments that these people somehow have come to know us intimately and that we too, are face to face with them. Here, for a while, we are.

Fintan O'Toole

IN SEARCH OF A BOOK

*T*he universe (which others call the Bookshop) is composed of an indefinite and perhaps infinite number of hexagonal galleries, with vast air shafts between, surrounded by very low railings. From any of the hexagons one can see, interminably, the upper and lower floors. The distribution of the galleries is invariable. Twenty shelves, five long shelves per side, cover all the sides except two: their height, which is the distance from floor to ceiling, scarcely exceeds that of a normal bookcase. One of the free sides leads to a narrow hallway which opens on to another gallery . . .

Like all those who love the bookshop, I have travelled in my youth; I have wandered in search of a book . . .

The passage with which I begin my personal reflection on the six-decade-old family business located on Galway's High Street that is celebrated in Ireland and abroad as Kennys Bookshop is taken, or rather (to use an expression for the practice favoured by Samuel Taylor Coleridge) 'filtered' from *The Library of Babel*, a lovingly-crafted tale written by one of the most extravagant book lovers of the twentieth century, Jorge Luis Borges.

In place of 'Library' I have substituted 'Bookshop'; and I have removed 'men of the Library' – not from any ludicrous considerations of that fashionable oxymoron, political correctness – and substituted 'those who love the bookshop'. And while my slight alterations may lack Senor Borges' felicity of expression, my warrant for engaging in this literary 'filtering' comes from Borges himself.

The great Argentinian author regarded the whole of creation as an endless text that is continually being written and rewritten, edited and annotated, annexed and dissolved, while the particular 'books' that stand or slope on the shelves of an infinity of libraries or bookshops, located in parallel spaces and times, are but one great palimpsest, carrying meanings and significations far more extensive and profound than any one reader or indeed army of readers could ever decipher. Yet the ever-receding goal is an irresistible bait, drawing the reader and collector deeper and deeper into this labyrinth.

The very first time I read *The Library of Babel*, many years past, I must have immediately and unconsciously made these substitutions. For when I re-read the story a few years ago, I was startled to see that what I had been carrying around in my memory as Borges' text was, in fact, a text that had been partially made my own. And the particular bookshop that I had in mind when I had originally read the tale was, of course, Kennys Bookshop: the bookshop as world.

For as long as I can remember I have loved bookshops. There are almost as many ways of accounting for this life-long passion as there are books in Kennys Bookshop. A bookshop is a place to browse, a place to meet friends and fellow-browsers, a place to strike up new friendships as, perhaps, you reach for a volume and discover someone else's hand racing you for its possession.

But one of the central attractions comes from the unstated but ever-present knowledge that any one of the books that fill the shelves may, in principle, become yours. Of course, financial considerations introduce very often the harsh note of reality; the pleasure with which I once lingered over, for example, a superb, leather-bound copy of Henry More's *Philosophical Writings*, the edition printed in 1652 by James Fletcher for William Morden Bookseller in Cambridge, was very much modified by the nagging awareness that I would most probably never have enough money to make it my own. Still, there was always the possibility. It is at moments like that that the purchase of a lottery ticket acquires a lustre it does not normally display.

Libraries, too, I have always loved, but with a different type of love, one not so warm as that I have instinctively given to bookshops. There was always something too public about libraries. And, what is more to the point, if I happened to fall in love with a particular book, there was always the irritating awareness that it would have to be given back at the end of a precisely specified period. Furthermore, there are few things that match the disappointment of looking up a title in the card catalogue, proceeding to the shelf where it allegedly awaits you, only to find that someone else has been there before you and removed it.

Libraries, then, are fine in their own way, but a bookshop is a place to pause, a place where time, which has become a merciless taskmaster to which we are nowadays all in thrall, is reappropriated by us, and we are able to 'take time', even to 'waste time', because it is once more ours. Before concluding this digression, I must mention a little-known fact: during the first few years of the existence of Kennys Bookshop, it also operated as a lending library. When I began writing this piece I was unaware of this, because that part of the business ceased operation long before I came to know the bookshop. However, in view of my 'filtered' Borges quotation, it is a happy coincidence that the most celebrated bookshop in Ireland was – for a time – also a library.

And so let me recapitulate: a great bookshop, like Kennys of Galway, is a universe, entire in itself. To wander through its rooms, pausing here to examine a well-thumbed copy of Kafka's *Castle* (itself a labyrinth), or over there to take up a lovingly-tended edition of Boswell's *Life of Johnson*, is a pleasure only those who have experienced it can fully appreciate. It has been my good fortune to know many great bookshops, and the discovery of each has marked an era in my travels through these distinct but filiated universes. However, my long and passionate affair with Kennys is the kind of love that happens but once in a lifetime.

A Family Affair

It began as a romance. Desmond Kenny, the son of *Connacht Tribune* editor Tom 'Cork' Kenny, his nickname indicating he came from the south, met Maureen Canning, a bright and attractive young girl who had won a scholarship, on her first day at University College Galway. Both came from book-loving families; Des's father dealt with words every day, and Des himself loved them passionately. The fact that his brother-in-law was the famous Galway writer and actor Walter Macken meant that literature was an integral part of his life. And Maureen, whose father had died when she was young, was raised by her book-loving and book-valuing mother. Books, in other words, were part of the context within which they grew to maturity. As soon as they had finished their studies, Des and Maureen married and decided to open a bookshop. Kennys Bookshop on High Street opened its doors to the public on 29 November 1940.

Today's enterprise boards, had they been in existence that November, would probably have politely suggested to the young couple that maybe they were letting their enthusiasm run ahead of their common sense. But, thank heavens, they were not around, and besides, it is unlikely that their prudent admonitions would have cut much ice in any case. Adventurous youth, back in the Irish 1940s, hadn't a lot to lose by taking chances.

Fortune was to favour Des and Maureen, if not immediately – those early years were tough – then certainly in the fullness of time. Most obviously it was to favour them with six children – four sons and two daughters: Thomas, Desmond Jr, Gerry, Jane, Monica, and Conor – who grew up in a world of books, a decisive early influence that has subsequently shaped each of their lives and which makes Kennys Bookshop & Gallery a family affair in a unique sense.

A Browser's Recollection

For almost thirty years now I have been cluttering up the passageways and aisles of the various establishments over which Maureen and her late husband Des have presided. One of the curious consequences of this lengthy 'semi-residency' (for even Kennys must sleep sometimes) is that whereas most people speak of Kennys Bookshop, I always think of Kennys *Bookshops*. For there have been several of them over the years. The first, of course, is the one everyone knows today. But thirty years ago, when I first walked through the door, the High Street premises consisted of only the front two, ground-floor rooms of the building. I was only to learn much later that, for roughly seven years, behind the book-lined walls, a number of newly-published editions of the Kenny family had been raised 'to the manor born', you might say. It was only in 1946 that the family moved to Salthill. And though the children were no longer obliged to share shelf space with the literary remains of authors, living and dead, rooms in the Salthill family home soon were handed over to an ever-expanding number of volumes for which there was no space in High Street.

One of my early memories of this temporary accommodation for new arrivals is of finding a copy of King James I's dotty treatise on witchcraft, a book that still sits on my bookshelves. Meanwhile, back in town, I watched the original bookshop expand and grow until it literally began to burst through the walls and – even more fascinatingly – through the ground floor. In 1969, the same year Gerry Kenny started his bookbinding apprenticeship in Dublin (which was to add yet one more dimension to the business); a decision to repair the old floorboards on the ground floor revealed a hitherto unknown basement or cellar of a good size. And to what use was this long-hidden space put? It was, of course, immediately shelved and filled with . . . books. (By the way, as you wander at will through the bookshop today, it might interest you to know that the front half of Kennys – that facing High Street – is actually what remains of one of the old town castles, dating from medieval times when Galway's merchants lived like princes. Around 1980, the old building disclosed more wonders – a priest's hole, where loyal Catholic families would shelter members of the clergy on the run from English 'priest-catchers'; and the magnificent fireplace on the first floor.)

To backtrack a few years to 1965, it was then that the premises at the corner of Cross Street and High Street opened, not as a bookshop but as an antique shop. Five years later, in 1970, the antiques disappeared and instead an Antiquarian Map & Print Shop was launched. Later, the Cross Street shop was the location for the annual second-hand book sale. At one of them I bought a complete set of Byron's *Works* and the six-volumes of Benjamin Jowett's edition of *Plato*. I was extremely happy going home that day, I can tell you.

However, the most magical of all the places where Kenny-acquired books found a temporary dwelling – from 1970 to 1981 – was on the upper floors of an old building on Upper Abbeygate Street. By now the influx of books – where they were all coming from we'll get to shortly – was becoming tidal, threatening to breach the hastily erected dykes on High Street. Before the entire building collapsed into the ground, or before customers would have to be admitted in single numbers only, the overflow of books needed a new home; hence Abbeygate Street. This was during the years in which it was used as a book depot, the most wonderful place in the world.

As I mentioned, the shop was located on the upper floors, and the glass-faced door was reached by way of a narrow staircase. Once you reached the tiny landing, you opened the door into a low-ceilinged set of rooms, all completely filled, of course, with shelves of books. Opening off this room was another, L-shaped room, dominated by a large desk. Behind it sat Des Kenny Sr, the joint publisher of the collected edition of the Kenny family. Des was not only a gentleman and a scholar, he was a wonderfully kind man, something I can attest to personally. He was also a profound bibliophile and I was most fortunate in the fact that he recognised in me a fellow spirit. And almost every time I visited the Abbeygate premises, he would show me some curious or rare volume that had come lately into his hands, and we would examine it together with that booklover's eloquent silence that was only broken by the occasional admiring remark. Having observed the necessary politenesses, he would return to what he had been doing before I entered, and I would then proceed into the wondrous labyrinth beyond.

I find it virtually impossible to give any just idea of what made these floors so special and so delightful. So I will simply try to describe what a typical visit was like, even while recognising how hopeless the attempt is for those who don't remember or have never experienced their wonders.

While the foyer and the room where Des Sr sat were nicely carpeted, heated and eminently presentable, once you turned into the L of this second room, beyond was bare floorboards, simple, knock-together shelving, and old and crumbling plastered walls. The aisles and passageways were narrow, twisting, and frequently so filled with massive stacks of bound volumes of *Household Words* or the *Edinburgh Review* that you had to climb over them, as if you were literally scaling the heights of Victorian literature.

And as you progressed further in, you discovered that there were several floors and two half-floors or mezzanines above you, reached by means of dangerous-looking, rickety staircases; if you chanced to look down as you were going up you realised instantly what your fate would be should you lose concentration. None of these rooms had any sort of heating, which was not a problem so long as the weather was fine. Come winter, however, and a visit to the Kenny attics sometimes resembled an expedition to the North Pole. But only if you happened to notice that sort of thing. Which is the same as saying, only if you were more conscious of your fingers and toes than you were of the heaps and mounds and dizzy ziggurats towering around you.

I can recall endless hours spent wandering up and down, in and out of these magical chambers, examining here an old edition of Carlyle's *Sartor Resartus*, or there an odd volume of Isaac Disraeli's *Curiosities of Literature*, lost in a delightful trance. With no windows to indicate the progress of the day, time ceased to have any meaning. I sometimes came to myself with no idea of how long I had been communing with the spirits of the mighty bound dead. In the winter, when I realised I had could no longer feel my toes, and found myself blowing on half-frozen fingers as I attempted to leaf through a copy of Sir Thomas Browne's *Religio Medici*, I knew it was time to head back downstairs. On those dark winter days, Des Sr would welcome me back to warmth with a very gratefully accepted steaming cup of tea. He kept a kettle on the boil to revive the frozen browser, rather in the same spirit animating the dispatch of the faithful St Bernard, his little keg of brandy tied beneath his pendulous dew-laps, the very sight of which is the sign of salvation for the lost Alpine climber.

Des Kenny Sr died in 1991. There is no way to measure such a loss to this close-knit family. He and Maureen had taken the gamble back in 1940 to open the bookshop. It took faith, sheer hard work and tenacity, and undoubtedly a goodly measure of luck to carry it off. Oh yes, and one or two other inestimable qualities that Des Sr possessed 'in spades', as the saying goes: integrity and a great and gentle charm.

Abbeygate Street was indeed a paradise. But, as with every paradise, it was not destined to last. And, of course, it did not make much sense to disperse the business in such a fashion. Kennys Bookshop, from the day it opened to the present day, is part of the fabric of High Street. And it was here that the next expansions were to take place. In 1979 the decision was taken to purchase the building on Middle Street which backed onto the original High Street premises. Indeed, in that same year the High Street premises were also purchased, having previously been rented. This allowed for the possibility of expansion upwards, as well as reconstruction and refurbishment.

A door was broken through from the back of the High Street building into the new establishment on Middle Street. And before the next major plan of expansion was set in motion, the large, bare room on Middle Street suddenly, inevitably, filled up with books. Not for long, though. Because this room, beautifully rebuilt and refurbished, became the Kenny Art Gallery in 1984. Yet the books kept arriving, year after year, as entire libraries were purchased from American universities. Another premises, this time on Merchants Road, was acquired in 1993 (additional storage space was added in 1995) to handle the enormous numbers of books arriving in Galway.

And so we come to 1996, and the single most ambitious expansion of the business ever undertaken. It was also the boldest. For it involved closing the bookshop entirely for a planned period of five months in order to completely rebuild and extend the interior of the now combined High Street/Middle Street premises. Miraculously, there were no disasters (and even a few more discoveries in the medieval fabric of the old building) and in June of 1996 John McGahern, an old friend of the Kenny family, officially re-opened the splendid new bookshop and gallery. Nicely, and very appropriately, coinciding with the advent of the new premises, Maureen Kenny was conferred with the degree of Master of Arts (*Honoris Causa*) by the National University of Ireland, Galway, for her contribution to the arts.

The Matriarch Herself

I have known Maureen Kenny for more than thirty years and during that time she has become a good friend. I have also increasingly come to respect her quiet strength, her kindness and consideration to one and all, her personal dignity and her extraordinary dedication to the culture of the book. Not to mention her tremendous sense of fun and her fluency in and love of the Irish language. Her influence on the business has been immeasurable.

As with all great bookshops and owners, Kennys has always been prepared to accommodate eccentricity. And so I remember an elderly man about whom nobody seemed to know very much, except that he was unquestionably learned. He wore a rather shabby raincoat and his shoes had certainly seen better days. I daresay in any other establishment had he been seen to linger or browse, he would have been escorted out the door pretty smartly. Maureen saw something in this elderly, rather defeated-looking man, and it touched her. So, without making anything of it, she had a chair placed near the particular shelves where he liked to browse –

sometimes for hours. And gradually a curious kind of friendship was born. She still knew nothing about him, except that he loved books, and that was enough.

When Maureen was conferred with an honorary degree the citation read at the ceremony summed up her contribution to the life of Galway over sixty years: *She and all she stands for remained a constant when virtually everything surrounding her had disappeared, been redeveloped, or surrendered to more perishable, transient tastes. Her metier represents one that is entwined with Galway's history and one which complements what we strive to achieve here at NUI Galway.*

The Pleasures of Publishing

The critic Walter Benjamin once remarked, 'Of all the ways of acquiring books, writing them oneself is regarded as the most praiseworthy method.' In that case, publishing the ones you wish to have is surely the next best method. Publishing was certainly not something the Kennys had ever originally considered as part of their plans. Walter Macken's *Oidhreacht na Mara*, published by Des and Maureen in 1944, was a one-off and was not followed by another publication for thirty years. And yet in the years between 1974 and 1994, an impressive list of new publications and distinguished reprints of older titles appeared under the Kenny imprint.

The first of the varied list began with William Hogan's collections, *Out of Season* (1978) and *Autumn Sequence* (1986). Others include *Nora Barnacle Joyce*, Padraic O'Laoi's pioneering biography of Joyce's Galway-born wife; Jeremiah Newman's *Maynooth and Victorian Ireland* (1983); Edmund Mahoney's delightful *Falcons & Foxhounds*, celebrating Galway's hunting tradition; Fr Martin Coen's important work of scholarship, *The Wardenship of Galway* (both 1984); Thomas Kenny's original and beautifully produced study of painter Kenneth Webb (1990); *Faces in a Bookshop*, (1990) in which a number of different artists portrayed a selection of the well-known literary visitors who have graced the bookshop over the years; *Down by the Claddagh*, Peadar O'Dowd's history of Galway's ancient fishing village (1993); Ivor Kenny's fascinating and perceptive book of interviews with noted Irish newspaper editors, *Talking to Ourselves* (1994), and *Galway, A Medico-Social History*, Dr James Murray's meticulously researched study of this surprisingly neglected dimension of Galway history.

Of equal importance in publishing history are the many essential and invaluable reprints of rare or out-of-print works on aspects of Galway history, the first of which was John Hardiman's *History of Galway* (1974). Others include Roderick O'Flaherty's *Iar Connacht* (1978); O'Sullivan's *Old Galway* (1983); Fahey's *History and Antiquities of the Diocese of Kilmacduagh* (1986), and the Rev. Patrick Egan's *The Parish of Ballinasloe* (1994).

Fine Binding

There is something very special and very beautiful about a finely-bound book. Indeed, we might say that in the hierarchy of the book, the aristocrats are those volumes which make their appearance in the resplendent attire of calfskin, goatskin, or even the humble cow. And so it was almost inevitable that one of the Kennys should take up the fine art of bookbinding. Fate or chance determined it was Gerry who took up the challenge. Originally located behind the family home in Salthill, the bindery is now situated in the new well-appointed headquarters of the Kenny export depot at the Liosbaun Estate on the outskirts of Galway. Gerry and his highly gifted professional co-workers bind all kinds of books, from battered old volumes with broken spines to brand-new books given the luxury treatment for collectors, libraries, gifts, or just for the person who appreciates the beauty and craftsmanship that once was part of the ordinary making of books. Each book, whether it be a copy of Joyce's *Ulysses* or an honourably outworn edition of *Mrs Beeton's Household Management*, is individually hand-crafted, from its stitched spine, laced cords and raised bands to its leather, buckram, or hand-marbled paper and 22 carat gold leaf lettering and decoration. Each, in short, is a work of art in its own right, even before you open the cover and begin reading.

Book Clubs and Websites

If you are unfortunate enough to live at a distance – the distance of an ocean, for example – from Kennys Bookshop, then acquiring the book or books you covet could present a problem. Kennys have undertaken to solve this problem for their customers and friends (in the establishment, the words are interchangeable) by way of their unique book club. It works like this: a selection of new Irish publications, hand-picked by Des Jr is made into a parcel or hamper and dispatched to anywhere in the world. All the books selected are sent on approval, so that if you decide that you don't really want *The Lost Distilleries of Ireland* (perhaps that was a bad example: who would not want *The Lost Distilleries of Ireland*? If only to go in search of them), you can exchange it for something more to your taste. Now, you might ask, how does Des know what to put in each hamper? The explanation is simple. In keeping with the entirely personal relationship that is so important between the bibliophile and Kennys, the customer is initially asked to provide an outline of his or her interests, and it is on the basis of this outline that the selections are made.

Although Kennys was already supplying its customers at home and abroad before the advent of the Internet, since 'going on-line', the possibilities for satisfying the range of individual customer choices has been extended and refined. An attractive feature of the Kenny website (http://www.kennys.ie) is 'Dessie's Diary', a chatty yet informed column where Des Jr talks about new Irish publications, talks to authors who have dropped into the shop recently, and provides an update on new developments in the business.

Book Exports

One of the fastest-developing subdivisions of the entire enterprise is the export business. It might come as something of a surprise to learn that Kennys is the largest and most important book exporter in Ireland. It is Conor who has taken over this side of things, having had a first-class initiation from his father. It didn't take Des Sr long to appreciate the considerable potential that existed for providing subject collections for various institutions around the world which would otherwise be forced to depend on the old unreliable method of 'hit-and-miss'. Earlier than most, Des, and then Conor, became aware of the fact that universities, for example, in Japan and the United States were anxious to build up subject collections for their libraries, especially, though not exclusively, of Irish publications. And so Conor, building on the instincts of his father, now oversees a complex export business in which, for example, a request from a Japanese university for a collection of books on the Industrial Revolution, or an

American university for a complete collection of publications by the writers associated with the Irish Literary Renaissance, will result, first, in the purchase of the entire stock of a large bookshop – and the particular shop may be anywhere around the world – followed by the careful cataloguing of the books into subjects, and finally the export of the specific collection requested to the particular library.

A concrete example will show the scale of the operation. Recently Conor received a request for a collection of 10,000 books on Africa. An intensive search of possible sources for such a collection led him to Hammersmith Books in England, which specialised in political publications. The result was the decision to purchase the entire stock of this old established bookshop – 200,000 books and approximately 50,000 political pamphlets.

Meeting Artists and Making Friends

From the very beginning, visual art and craftwork were to feature prominently in the growth and evolution of what was to become Kennys Bookshop and Gallery. In 1951 Kennys hosted an exhibition of handcrafted rugs by Joan Fretwell, and the following year the first exhibition of ceramics by Nell Murphy. As early as 1953, an artist who was not only to show his work on a regular basis at Kennys but was also to become a good friend had his first exhibition. I refer, of course, to Kenneth Webb. Forty years later, Thomas's beautifully illustrated study of the artist set the seal on this unique relationship. In 1968 Des and Maureen knocked out the living room, dining room, and hall, of their home in Salthill and opened the first gallery in the West of Ireland. Finally, as we have already seen, the gallery moved in 1984 to Middle Street.

While I have no wish to subject readers to long lists of names, nonetheless, it is important for the story I am telling that some of the artists should be mentioned in order to illustrate the quality of artistic work that has been shown in the gallery over the years. And so I offer a small sample of these: Paul Henry, Sean Keating, Raymond Piper, John Behan, Birgitta Hummel, Patricia Cockburn, Brian Bourke, Sean McSweeney, George Campbell, Arthur Armstrong, Derek Biddulph, John Coll, Susan Webb, Gertrude Degenhardt, Hugh McCormick, and Joseph Quilty.

In addition to individual shows, the gallery has hosted many group and theme events; among them an exhibition of press photographs in 1956 entitled Germany: Ten Years After the War; Interpretations of Dante's Divine Comedy, an exhibition of forty-three living Irish artists sponsored by the Italian Cultural Institute (1958); the work of the Kilkenny Design Workshops, the work of Irish Women Artists, and an exhibition of the work of Galway photographers (all in 1975); work from the Regional Technical College Art Department (1980); the Faces in a Bookshop exhibition (1990); Music and Musicians (1992, coinciding with Galway Arts Festival); On the Subject of Drink (1993, also for Galway Arts Festival); an exhibition of the work of graduates of the Art Department of the RTC; and, for the last few Christmases, A Magic Room in Galway.

Exhibition openings are an occasion for celebration. Picture a large and airy room, the walls painted a brilliant white. This is the exhibition space, the warm, welcoming atmosphere which Tom Kenny has laboured to perfect. Now I have to say that, even in a country blessed with witty and word-crazy people, Tom Kenny stands out. The deliciously puckish expression on his face as he rolls into a story or tells a joke, the undisguised affection he has for the artists who exhibit in the gallery, and his knowledge, worn lightly, of the great kingdom of art itself are part of the charm he displays on such occasions. With his few, well-chosen words out of the way, he introduces the guest speaker. And because of the bookshop and the long association the Kennys have had with just about every important cultural figure in Ireland, the range of speakers is very impressive.

As a result, I have listened to much eloquence in this room over the years: the poet and author of *Anam Cara*, John O'Donohue, actress Fionnuala Flanagan, the several bishops of Galway, former Cultural Minister and poet Michael D. Higgins, and former president of Ireland Dr Patrick Hillery, to Dr Noel Browne, the Knight of Glin, playwright and author Hugh Leonard, and the great actress Siobhan McKenna. Finally, the artist is invited to say a few words. I stress 'few words' because most artists are only too happy to let their work speak for them. Yet eloquence is evident here also: renowned sculptor John Behan; that fine artist, the late Hugh McCormick, and the delightful 'Burren artist', the late Joseph Quilty. Again the list could be extended.

And perhaps before we leave the subject of good company and the hundreds of faces in the bookshop and gallery, I could produce a few of my most memorable snapshots, such as standing beside the legendary American poet Allen Ginsberg in one of the upstairs rooms; taking the late Patrick Lindsay away from the shop into a nearby pub for an interview; meeting Seamus Heaney; listening to *Angela's Ashes* author Frank McCourt charm Mrs Kenny; watching as Catherine Kennedy and Anne De Winton, Lady Gregory's two granddaughters, examine first editions of their grandmother's books, and laughing uproariously as poet and essayist Tom Lynch (whose 'day job' is undertaker in a small Michigan town) describes how other poets react when he tells them what he does 'for a living'.

The Photographs

And so to the photographs. Between the covers of this book are many faces of many different people, living and dead. They include poets and playwrights, painters and politicians, novelists and (at least one) navy man, singers and actors, historians and publishers, and a few who might be described, in the best possible sense, unclassifiable. Some have an international reputation, many have shaped Irish cultural life over the past decades, the impact of others has been more local; however, they all have one thing in common: they all, at one time or another, have paid a visit to Kennys Bookshop and Gallery.

If you wanted to be a bit mischievous, when it comes to the question of fame, you could look at it from two, overlapping, points of view. The subjects of the photographs in this book a) were famous when they entered Kennys, or, b) considering the fame of Kennys, they are famous because they called into Kennys. In either case, fame surrounds them all like a genial aura.

Here we have the authentic, original Kenny Collection, a collection that's been growing since the earliest days of the bookshop, when it was, as my daughter used to say, only this big. How did it come about? Was there a grand plan? Had the frames already been purchased? Was the camera ready and loaded for action from Day One? Hardly. Like so many brilliant ideas, the origins of the Kenny Portrait Gallery can be located in the domain of the goddess of happenstance. According to Tom Kenny, it took a few visits by the Grim Reaper to concentrate the mind. Apparently it was the demise of the likes of Brendan Behan, Kate O'Brien, and Walter Macken to sound the wake-up call. Here you had a couple of Ireland's finest writers who spent their shillings in the shop and now – to put it with the greatest of tact – they wouldn't be doing so anymore. Why didn't we get their photographs?

On a platform as makeshift and improvised as this, the Kenny Collection was born. In the early days, if a notable writer, artist, or whatever crossed the threshold, somebody would race across the street to Ray Shanley, who used to have a photographic studio opposite the shop entrance on High Street, or round up Yann, whose studio was around the corner on Mainguard Street, or ring up Jimmy Walsh of the *Connacht Tribune,* and they would drop everything and come running, camera in hand. Click-snap, and the job was done. After a while, however, it dawned on the assembled Kennys that it might be much easier – certainly much easier on Ray Shanley, at least – if one of them got behind the shutter and took the photographs. And so it happens that Monica, who has become a fine portrait photographer, is responsible for the majority of the photographs in this collection. Of course I am treating with considerable brevity and, indeed, levity the stages by which all of this was accomplished. But the main fact of it is, that over the years one of the most famous 'sites' in Galway has also displayed some of the most famous 'sightings' to visit the City of the Tribes and, more especially, Kennys Bookshop and Gallery.

Needless to say the images included in this book are only a small and rather arbitrary selection from the quite awesome photographic archive assembled by Kennys over the past four or five decades. For ease of reference the subjects have been arranged in alphabetical order. This means that there is no particular chronological or hierarchical sequence to their inclusion, so that photographs taken in the 1960s and 1970s lie alongside more recent portraits. However, Gabrielle Warnock's in-depth biographies provide an invaluable context for the faces that gaze out from the following pages.

Jeff O'Connell

PORTRAITS
IN A BOOKSHOP

BELLA AKHMADULINA

Our photograph is a bit of a coup. She doesn't normally smile in photographs. I wasn't aware of this, but I thought she was looking a bit gloomy, so I stood behind Monica and pulled my ears and stuck my tongue out and she cracked up! (Kennys)

JOHN ARDEN

MARGARET ATWOOD

SEBASTIAN BARRY

The complete artist, and a promoter, supporter, encourager of young artists. (Kennys)

JOHN BEHAN

SARA BERKELEY

His words became his actions; poetry of truth issued in non-violent protest against war; immersed in the prophetic call of the Bible he, with others, wrote new chapters of that peaceable Kingdom. (Pat O'Brien)

DANIEL BERRIGAN

*She never stops talking –
but she never stops
listening either.* (Kennys)

MAEVE BINCHY

EAVAN BOLAND

*The publisher three times
retired. He's the reason
Francis Stuart came back
into print. Another of the
great celebrators. (Kennys)*

DERMOT BOLGER

PAT BORAN

CLARE BOYLAN

He was a regular. He opened several exhibitions, launched many books. He was a generous promoter of young artists and writers. (Kennys)

NOEL BROWNE

BILL BRYSON

GEORGE CAMPBELL
with Des and Maureen Kenny

His funeral was attended by a huge number of young artists, an eloquent testament to his art, his influence and his generosity. (Kennys)

Growing up in Donegal,
I reached the age of
fourteen before I realised
that sarcasm was not one
of the martial arts.
(Moya Cannon)

MOYA CANNON

CIARÁN CARSON

PHILIP CASEY

ANNE CHAMBERS

She has returned her true identity to Grace O'Malley. (Kennys)

It's Jung Chang's mother that I really remember. She had no English and my mother has no Chinese, but the communication between them was amazing. (Kennys)

JUNG CHANG

BRENDAN CLEARY

HARRY CLIFTON AND DEIRDRE MADDEN

A true bibliophile. One of those people who gets lost in a bookshop. (Kennys)

SIR JAMES COMYN

SHANE CONNAUGHTON

DON CONROY

TIM PAT COOGAN

ANTHONY CRONIN

MARGARETTA D'ARCY

ROALD DAHL

'No child must be disappointed' was his main instruction
before a three-day signing session. No child was! A genius
with children. (Kennys)

Bubbling with energy and enthusiasm, one of the great promoters of Irish literature in the U.S. (Kennys)

ADELE DALSIMER

ITA DALY AND DAVID MARCUS

MICHAEL DAVITT with his son, Joe

GERALD DAWE

*Connemara's accolade is to call his son
'Mac an Dictionary'.* (Kennys)

TOMÁS DE BHALDHRAITHE (LEFT)
with Tomás Laighleis and Daithi Ó Uaithne

LOUIS DE PAOR
with Fionnuala and their children

The black and white photo does not do justice to this glorious crop of redheads. (Kennys)

Two literary ladies, intensely proud of their heritage. (Kennys)

ANNE DE WINTON AND
CATHERINE KENNEDY

JOHN F. DEANE

*What I love about the West
is the space . . . to feel the
fresh air, to feel the gorse
and heather under your
feet, the wind and the rain
in your face . . .*
(G. Degenhardt)

GERTRUDE DEGENHARDT

FRANK DELANEY

GREG DELANTY with his wife, Patti

DON DELILLO

MICHEL DÉON with his wife, Chantal

EILÍS DILLON

J. P. DONLEAVY

KATIE DONOVAN

THEO DORGAN

SEÁN DUNNE

PAUL DURCAN

Ellman was an extraordinarily generous man with his talents. When we were publishing Father Paddy Lee's biography of Nora Barnacle, he had the manuscript returned to us within ten days, fully annotated. (Kennys)

RICHARD ELLMAN

EMYR ESTYN EVANS with his wife, Gwyneth

PETER FALLON

BERNARD FARRELL

Gave a memorable reading at the launch of his collected poems in Kennys in 1996. (Kennys)

PADRAIC FIACC

GABRIEL FITZMAURICE with his wife, Brenda

MICHAEL FLAHERTY

His father and Nuala Ní Dhomhnaill's mother used to cycle to dances together – on the same bicycle. (Kennys)

JOHN FLANAGAN

TOM FLANAGAN

RICHARD FORD

FREDERICK FORSYTH

BRIAN FRIEL

BRENDAN FULLAM with his wife and his daughter

PATRICK GALVIN

ALLEN GINSBERG

On his first visit to the shop Ginsberg, ignoring all the brou-ha-ha around him, scanned the shelves closely. Finding an obviously artificial binding, curiosity got the better of him. He opened it to find a secret closet inside. 'Hmm,' he muttered. 'What a lovely place to hide your marijuana!' (Kennys)

Michael is one of the few poets who 'gives out' his poetry without reference to the text. He believes that 'poetry should be recited, not read'. (Kennys)

MICHAEL GORMAN

EAMONN GRENNAN with daughter, Kira

GERALD HANLEY

EOGHAN HARRIS

TONY HARRISON

MICHAEL HARTNETT

FRANCIS HARVEY

His description of a half-day in Cavan has resonances for anyone who grew up in a small Irish town. (Kennys)

DERMOT HEALY

Michael Finlan dropped the manuscript (Nineteen Acres) *on my father's desk with an imperative 'Read this!' Within ten minutes, father was crying and telling us we were going to publish it.* (Kennys)

JOHN HEALY

SEAMUS HEANEY

AIDAN HIGGINS

RITA ANN HIGGINS

JUDITH AND JEREMIAH HOAD

DESMOND HOGAN

MÁIRE HOLMES

Like St Luke – a healer and a poet. (Kennys)

MIROSLAV HOLUB

To Tom Kenny, With best wishes, and in the hope that your son a) lets you read Fever Pitch *and b) sees the error of his ways (i.e. not being an Arsenal fan.* (Nick Hornby, The Visitors' Book)

GARRY HYNES

I can still see him trying to make a gallery full of children look up
their noses – and almost succeeding. (Kennys)

PAT INGOLDSBY

HIRO ISHIBASHI

P. D. JAMES AND RUTH RENDELL

FRED JOHNSTON

JENNIFER JOHNSTON

First time I ever clapped
eyes on Neil was when two
lads (himself and Des
Hogan) appeared in the
shop with their books
under their arms and asked
my mother would she stock
them. She took the lot.
One of the books was
Night in Tunisia, *the other,*
The Ikon Maker. *They've
been known in here as 'the
two lads' ever since.*
(Kennys)

NEIL JORDAN

JOHN B. KEANE
with his wife, Mary

*With those báinín men I'm
one!* (Seán Keating)

SEÁN KEATING

Here is where I found all the pictures and all the forms that fed me in my empty cell. Many thanks. (Brian Keenan, The Visitors' Book)

BRIAN KEENAN

JIM KEMMY

THOMAS KENEALLY with his wife, Judy

WILLIAM KENNEDY with his wife, Dana

Fun and antics. He's playful, wordful. (Kennys)

BRENDAN KENNELLY

An Omagh original – the 'Gobán Saor' of the twentieth century. (Kennys)

BENEDICT KIELY

TOM KILROY

BILL KING AND ANITA LESLIE

THOMAS KINSELLA

PASCAL L'ESTRANGE

MARY LAVIN

*An outstanding storyteller
who puts enormous energy
and personality into his art.*
(Kennys)

EDDIE LENIHAN

HUGH LEONARD

DENISE LEVERTOV

If there was a man to shorten a journey, Pat Lindsay was one. (Kennys)

PATRICK LINDSAY

MORGAN LLYWELYN

LIZ LOCHHEAD

EDNA LONGLEY with daughter, Sarah

MICHAEL LONGLEY

THOMAS LYNCH

When launching his book of essays, The Undertaking, *he presented me with a ring in the shape of a coffin that opened. 'The symbolism' he said to me 'is not unlike the Claddagh Ring. The coffin always goes into the church head first, so if you see someone wearing this ring with the head facing the nail, you know his number is up'.* (Kennys)

A shy man who felt his photograph should not hang in a bookshop.
(Kennys)

DÓNALL MAC AMLAIGH

LIAM MAC CON IOMAIRE with his wife, Bairbre

PROINSIAS MAC AONGHUSA

GEORGE MACBETH

TOM MACINTYRE

WALTER MACKEN
with his wife, Peggy

He was in here three or four times a week. He almost lived in the place. Did all his research in here. (Kennys)

BERNARD MACLAVERTY

MacLean and Padraic Fiacc combined to give an extraordinary poetry reading in our gallery in Salthill during the late 1970s. The reading was extraordinary for the way the two poets, who worked in techniques so far apart, gelled so superbly together in front of a packed gallery. (Kennys)

SORLEY MACLEAN

BRYAN MACMAHON

JAYANTA MAHAPATRA

DEREK MAHON

EAMONN MALLIE

DAVID MALOUF

MARY MANNING

AUGUSTINE MARTIN

EUGENE MCCABE
with his wife, Margot

Sitting at the bottom of the garden chatting when the gardener, pointing up a landway, suddenly said: "They went that way!" McCabe, the storyteller, asked "Who went that way?". Thus was Death and Nightingales *born.* (Kennys)

A good listener who can sit for hours and then puts everything in a nutshell of three or four words. He likes to test people's imagination, using the macabre as a satiric weapon to attack modern mores. (Kennys)

PAT MCCABE

NELL MCCAFFERTY

COLUM MCCANN

THOMAS MCCARTHY

TOM MCCAUGHREN with his daughters

MIKE MCCORMACK

Appreciates the work being done for him in bookshops. You really feel he's grateful. Hasn't lost the head with all the success. Very down to earth. (Kennys)

FRANK MCCOURT

BREEGE MCCUSKER

MARTIN MCDONAGH

VINCENT MCDONNELL with his wife, Joan

There is nothing as intimate as the relationship that exists between the reader and book during the act of reading. (Paraphrase of a statement made in his speech opening the refurbished Kennys Bookshop.)

JOHN MCGAHERN

MEDBH MCGUCKIAN

FRANK MCGUINNESS

*Sonas ar mo chuid cáirde
go léir, agus ar mo
námhaid má táid ann!*
(Siobhán McKenna)

SIOBHÁN MCKENNA

PAULA MEEHAN

My abiding memory of M.J. is of him shuffling into the shop carrying his battered briefcase. There'd be a hushed conversation between Mother and himself, during which she would buy, and pay for, two or three copies of each of his plays. I always thought it was a savage indictment of Irish publishing that a playwright as important as Molloy should have to peddle his wares from door to door. (Kennys)

M. J. MOLLOY

Poetry is the whiskey of the brain
Prose the stout.
Let them both pour out!
(John Montague)

JOHN MONTAGUE

BRIAN MOORE

Knowing Christy for two minutes is as if he had been a friend all your life and you definitely become his. (Kennys)

CHRISTY MOORE

PAUL MULDOON with his wife, Jean, and daughter, Dorothy

MICHAEL MULLEN

DERVLA MURPHY

Her trip to Galway for Cúirt was by bicycle and bus. She wouldn't dream of putting another car on the road to collect her. And as for staying in a hotel when a nice Irish family home was in the neighbourhood! (Kennys)

. . . a gentleman and a gentle man. (Paddy Henry)

JOHN MURPHY

RICHARD MURPHY

When asked for an epitome on poetry, Murphy thought for a minute, laughed and said 'As the tinker wife says of her husband, he gets us out of one disaster into another much worse'. (Kennys)

The playscript on his lap is Bailegangaire *just before going into rehearsal with Garry Hynes.* (Kennys)

TOM MURPHY

LES MURRAY

EILÉAN NÍ CHUILLEANÁIN

I always associate Nuala with laughter – throwing her head back and laughing. A straight-talking woman. (Kennys)

NUALA NÍ DHOMHNAILL

SIDNEY NOLAN

JOE NOONAN

CONOR CRUISE O'BRIEN AND MÁIRE MHAC AN tSAOI

Writers! Now Joyce! Now, there's a writer! Why a page of Joyce a day is like a transfusion!
(Edna O'Brien)

EDNA O'BRIEN

A true poet of the people. (Kennys)

PATRICK O'BRIEN

JULIE O'CALLAGHAN

JOE O'CONNOR

ULICK O'CONNOR

MARY O'DONNELL with her daughter, Anna

*When handed a first
edition of* Islanders *to sign,
O'Donnell said 'That book
wrote itself. To keep my
sanity, I composed it in
solitary confinement and
then wrote it with the first
pencil and paper I could lay
my hands on in one
straight draft'.* (Kennys)

PEADAR O'DONNELL

His philosophical and poetic meditations on Celtic spirituality have thrown a luminous hope to people living in the darkness of this century's politics and economics.
(Pat O'Brien)

JOHN O'DONOHUE

DENNIS O'DRISCOLL

O'Flaherty was curiously shy about his work. Whenever she knew he was in town, Mother would fill the window with his books. He never called in although Mother says she is sure she often caught him at the window. It was he who introduced Breandán Ó hEithir to the shop. (Kennys)

LIAM O'FLAHERTY

LARRY O'LOUGHLIN

*She's all the time working
at her craft. She knows the
limits and she knows the
possibilities.* (Kennys)

MARY O'MALLEY

MICHEAL O'SIADHAIL

The higher the art, the fewer the gestures. (Ben Okri, The Visitors' Book)

BEN OKRI

FRANK ORMSBY

LEARAÍ Ó FÍNNEADHA

BRENDÁN Ó hEITHIR

The conscience of the Gaeltacht. (Kennys)

SEÁN Ó MORDHA

LIAM Ó MUIRTHILE

Cathal Ó Sándair, m'athair agus mo Gaiscíoch, I salute you.
(Tarloch Ó Sándair)

CATHAL Ó SÁNDAIR

CATHAL Ó SEARCAIGH

SEÁN Ó TUAMA

JOSÉ EMILIO PACHECO

JAMES PLUNKETT

NICHOLAS AND MARY ROBINSON

Known throughout Connemara as 'Fear Na Mapaí'. (Kennys)

TIM ROBINSON

A shy person. Most at home when he's on the stage. (Kennys)

BILLY ROCHE

JAMES RYAN, CAROLINE WALSH with Alice and Matt

JOHN RYAN

MAINCHÍN SEOIGHE

JAMES SIMMONS AND JANICE FITZPATRICK SIMMONS with Ben

GARY SNYDER

FRANCIS STUART

Modest and very generous with her time, even at the height of To School Through The Fields *when she was being pulled every way by every one.* (Kennys)

ALICE TAYLOR

D. M. THOMAS

COLM TÓIBÍN

On her way in to hospital, she stopped, looking for something to read, and was photographed. (Kennys)

HONOR TRACY

Trained to be a sculptor,
but once, after chipping
away at a block of wood
until there was nothing
left, he went to Michael
and Frances Biggs and said
'I'll never be a sculptor, so
I'm going to take up
writing instead.' (Kennys)

WILLIAM TREVOR

ZDENEK URBÁNEK with his daughter

Voznesensky read at Cúirt to a packed audience. Despite the fact that he read only in Russian it is still remembered by some as the best poetry reading they had ever heard. (Kennys)

ANDREI VOZNESENSKY

DEREK WALCOTT

A sense of place is the most important element in his work.
That place, his spiritual home, is Ballinaboy, near Clifden.
(Kennys)

KENNETH WEBB

DAVID WHEATLEY

BIOGRAPHIES

BELLA AKHMADULINA 1937–

Born in Moscow. Attended the Gorky Literary Institute. Although admitted to the Soviet Writer's Union, her work attracted official criticism and she had difficulty getting it published. The first of several marriages was to Yevgeny Yevtushenko in the 1950s. Her first collection, *Struna* (The Harp String), appeared in 1962. 'Classical in form and not unrelated to the Acmeist tradition, her poetry moves among scenes of the concrete world, described with precision and gentle irony.' (Dimitri Obolensky, *The Heritage of Russian Verse*) F.D. Reeve published a translation of her new and selected poems in *The Garden* in 1990. In this collection it is revealed that flowers, a recurring theme in her earlier work, 'act simultaneously as the source of inspiration as well as its result – the poems themselves.' (Christine Rydel, *Contemporary World Writers*) She has translated poetry from Georgian and other languages. Greatly respected as one of the 'Thaw' poets of the 1950s. In the climate of hostility towards artists which followed, she suffered a period of drought (rain is used by her as a symbol for poetic inspiration), but in the 1970s her poems began to appear again regularly. Her collected works were published to coincide with her sixtieth birthday.

JOHN ARDEN 1930–

' . . . modern dramatists must attempt two apparently contradictory tasks. 1) They must abandon their solitary status and learn to combine together to secure conditions-of-work and artistic control over the products of their imagination. 2) They must be prepared to combine not only with their fellows, but also with *actors*. It is not enough for the occasional author to *direct*; playwrights should be members of theatrical troupes, and take part in all aspects of production.' (Arden, quoted in *Contemporary Dramatists*) Has devoted much of his writing career to working in collaboration with his wife, Margaretta D'Arcy, with whom he has written numerous plays, such as *The Non-Stop Connolly Show* and *Vandaleur's Folly*, which 'not only confront community issues but are often the product of community cooperation. Thus, both form and content reflect the socio-political commitments of their collaborators'. (Elaine Turner, *Contemporary Dramatists*) Some of his early plays, such as *Live Like Pigs* (produced London, New York), *Serjeant Musgrave's Dance* (London, San Francisco, New York) and *Armstrong's Last Goodnight* (Glasgow, London, Boston) are seen as seminal works. Novels include *Silence Among the Weapons*, *Books of Bale*, *Jack Juggler and the Emperor's Whore*. From Yorkshire, he has lived in Galway for many years.

MARGARET ATWOOD 1939–

Canada's foremost novelist, poet and critic was born in Ottawa. Her father was an entymologist and much of her childhood was spent in the northern Ontario and Quebec wilderness. She graduated from the University of Toronto and has taught English literature at several Canadian universities. She has also travelled extensively, in America, Europe and Australia. Her first book of poetry, *The Circle Game*, won the Governor-General's Award when it was published in 1966. Her first novel, *The Edible Woman*, was published in 1969. Three of her novels, *The Handmaid's Tale*, *Cat's Eye* and *Alias Grace* (a haunting recreation of the enigmatic Grace, convicted, with her lover, for the murder of her employer during the nineteenth century), have been shortlisted for the Booker Prize and she has received numerous awards for both her fiction and her poetry. *The Handmaid's Tale*, which won both the Arthur C. Clarke Award for Science Fiction and the Governor-General's Award, was also made into a film, scripted by Harold Pinter and starring Faye Dunaway, Robert Duvall and Aidan Quinn. Her short story collections include *Wilderness Tips*.

SEBASTIAN BARRY 1955–

'In these luminous plays, the drama comes, not from public conflicts, but from the human dignity that survives the loss of public meanings . . . Grace and disgrace, for instance, are constant companions. Sebastian Barry fills the stage with prodigal people, long lost to the wider world . . . men and women defeated and discarded by their times.' (Fintan O'Toole) Barry, son of actress Joan O'Hara, was born in Dublin and educated in Trinity College. Has lived mainly outside Ireland since 1977. *The Steward of Christendom*, first produced in London, won numerous awards. *Our Lady of Sligo,* its companion play, was very well-received in New York this year, particularly for the performance of Sinead Cusack as Mai O'Hara. 'Ms Cusack's Mai makes it clear that not all natural stars wind up on stages or screens. Trapped in what they see as lesser lives, they are destroyed by their own fire, but they still burn bright,' (Ben Brantley, the *New York Times*). Other plays include *Boss Grady's Boys* (1989), *Prayers of Sherkin* (1991), *The Only True History of Lizzie Finn,* and *White Woman Street* (1995). Has published several poetry collections, while *The Whereabouts of Eneas McNulty* is his first novel since the late 1980s.

JOHN BEHAN 1938–

'Say the name of Dante and you think of the circles of Hell or the brilliant light-filled spheres of his Paradiso . . . Say the name John Behan and you see the bulls of Cooley and the Children of Lir and the bittern of Cathal Bui, the birds of Aengus, and now, after this exhibition, the boats of Broighter and the Ostfold boat and the ghost boat and even the boar of Ben Bulben . . . Behan has made a mark in our collective imagination . . .'. (Seamus Heaney, opening 'Oriental Occidental' at Kenny's Gallery, 1998) Behan was born in Dublin. Studied in Dublin, London and Oslo. Instrumental in establishing the Project Arts Centre in 1967 and the Dublin Art Foundry in 1970. One of Ireland's leading artists. He works in bronze, aluminium, steel and brass. Principal commissions include *Train Panel*, Gresham Hotel, *Megalithic Memory*, AIB Centre, Dublin, *Turfcutter*, Bord na Mona H.Q., Dublin, *Swan Monument*, Cork and *Twin Spires,* NUI, Galway. In 1997 former President, Mary Robinson, unveiled Behan's national monument to the Great Famine, a bronze coffin ship at the foot of Croagh Patrick.

SARA BERKELEY 1967–

Berkeley's first collection of poems, *Penn*, published when she was a nineteen-year old student at Trinity College, was shortlisted for the *Irish Times* award for poetry in 1986. Since then, Dublin-born Berkeley has published two further volumes of verse, *Home Movie Nights* (1989) and *Facts about Water: New and Selected Poems* (1995). *The Swimmer in the Deep Blue Dream* (1991) is a collection of short stories. Her poetry 'has been likened to eastern European verse written after World War II. As a delver into shadow areas of human consciousness, Berkeley has few equals among Irish poets of her generation.' (*Modern Irish Lives*) Her first novel, *Shadowing Hannah*, explores the disturbing psychological aftermath of a consenting incestuous relationship between a brother and sister. The novel, which grew out of an already published short story because she 'couldn't let the characters go' (to Rosita Boland, *The Irish Times*), was published last year. She lives in California, where she has worked for some years as a technical writer, writing computer manuals. She recently went freelance and is writing a second novel.

DANIEL BERRIGAN 1921–

'Because we want peace with half a heart and half a life and will, the war, of course, continues, because the waging of war, by its nature, is total – but the waging of peace, by our own cowardice, is partial. So a whole will and a whole heart and a whole national life bent towards war prevail over the mere desire for peace.' (quoted by Fintan O'Toole, *The Irish Times*) Social activist and poet, the USA Jesuit priest, Daniel Berrigan, has waged peace throughout his life. In the 1960s, he opposed the Vietnam War. Jailed in 1970 for destroying draft registration files in Catonsville, Maryland. In 1971 the Berrigan brothers were successfully defended by the lawyer Paul O'Dwyer (New York Democrat, who died in 1998) against a charge of plotting to kidnap Henry Kissinger. Arrested frequently during the 1980s for protests at weapons manufacturers and other sites. In the late 1990s, Nobel Peace Prizewinner, Mairead Maguire (Corrigan), proposed the Berrigan brothers for the Nobel Peace Prize. Has written more than fifty books, including *Night Flight to Hanoi* (1968), *The Trial of the Catonsville Nine* (1970), poetry books and an autobiography.

MAEVE BINCHY 1940–

Maeve is so well known, not only through her tremendously popular books, but also through her Saturday column in *The Irish Times,* that a biographical sketch seems almost redundant. She was born in 1940, grew up in Dublin and went to University College, Dublin. She taught for several years before becoming a journalist with *The Irish Times*. She loves her own characters, she's interested in them and she feels for them. 'Binchy's willingness to acknowledge in her novels a sense of a world without purpose . . . creates a dense picture of Irish life in the 1950's and 1960's'. (Karen Robertson, *Contemporary Novelists*). Starting with *Light a Penny Candle,* her career has gone from strength to strength. Some of her novels have been adapted for film. *Tara Road* was chosen for Oprah Winfrey's Book Club and quarter of a million copies were sold in the month before the studio discussion. 'If I told anybody [in advance of the announcement], the whole thing would be off,' Binchy told Paddy Kehoe (*RTÉ Guide*). She has written several plays, and her television play *Deeply Regretted By* won two Jacob's Awards and the Best Script Award at the Prague Film Festival.

EAVAN BOLAND 1944–

'I don't accept that womanhood is a state we can somehow historically transcend. It is a human condition, not a historic one and as such is a very rich, central part of imagination, not only of social consciousness.' (Boland to Eileen Battersby, *The Irish Times*) Her father was an ambassador and though born in Dublin Boland spent large periods of her childhood in London and New York. When she returned to Dublin as a teenager, her sense of location had been ruptured and she was left feeling an outsider. She developed as a highly intense and intellectual poet whose poetry illuminates the familiar. Her collections of poetry include *New Territory* (published when she was twenty-two), *The War Horse, In Her Own Image* and *Night Feed*. In 1971 she co-wrote *WB Yeats and his World* with Micheál MacLiammóir. Won a Macaulay Fellowship for poetry (1968). She is Professor of English at Stanford University and directs the Stanford Creative Writing Programme. Later work includes *The Journey, An Origin Like Water – Collected Poems 1967-1987* and *Outside History* (1990). In 1995 she published an 'outstanding' memoir, *Object Lessons,* 'which is as much a powerfully argued, evocatively-written poetic manifesto as autobiography' (Battersby). Published *The Lost Land* in 1998.

DERMOT BOLGER 1959–

His Raven Arts Press, founded in 1977, gave a platform to many new writers, such as Pat McCabe, Sara Berkeley and Paul Durcan. It also championed the works of Francis Stuart – 'one of only a handful of twentieth century Irish writers that I can imagine future generations embracing' (to Robert O'Byrne, *The Irish Times*), – publishing eleven of his books during its existence. He subsequently founded New Island Books. As well as being a publisher, he is a writer of substance. His play, *The Lament for Arthur Cleary,* won the Samuel Beckett Award, the BBC Stewart Parker Award and an Edinburgh Fringe First Award. A recent play, *The Passion of Jerome*, mixing reality with the surreal, appeared in February 1999. Books include *The Journey Home, The Woman's Daughter, Night Shift*. One of his most entertaining (and successful) enterprises in recent years was the devising of *Finbar's Hotel*, a novel in which each chapter was written by a different writer. The reader's job is to guess the identity of each writer. The game has been sufficiently intriguing to warrant the book's publication in seven languages (including Serbian). And then there is the poetry – five collections.

PAT BORAN 1963–

Boran's first collection of poetry, *The Unwound Clock*, won the Patrick Kavanagh Award in 1989. 'A medley of self-obsessed voices is set in motion, and a tense inner drama, or series of dramas unfolds in a mood reminiscent of the atmosphere of an ensemble by Munch or Strindberg. It is an uncanny, utterly absorbing work . . .' (*Poetry Ireland Review*) This was followed by two further collections, *Familiar Things* (1993) and *The Shape of Water* (1996). A collection of short stories, *Strange Bedfellows*, appeared in 1991. Boran has written for a variety of audiences. Non-fiction includes *A Short History of Dublin*. As K.S. Daly, he wrote two books, *Ireland, an Encyclopedia for the Bewildered* and *Sex, an Encyclopedia for the Bewildered*. Produced a book for children, *All the Way to China* (1998). *The Portable Creative Writing Workshop* (Salmon Publishing) provides practical advice on starting to write. Conducts writing workshops in schools, colleges and prisons, as well as for writers' groups. Runs an online course for poets and fiction writers. Has been writer-in-residence at many institutions. Was editor of *Poetry Ireland Review*. Presented the RTÉ television books programme, 'Undercover'.

CLARE BOYLAN 1948–

Boylan is a highly regarded novelist and short story writer. *Holy Pictures*, published in 1983, was widely praised. '[A] skilfully-achieved creation, Boylan's outwardly simple style concealing the depth of her insights. Visual imagery is subtly but continually used throughout the book – family photographs, pictures of film stars, the religious cards that give the novel its title . . . together, they provide a series of ikons which serve as a focus for the dreams and longings of the characters.' (Geoff Sadler, *Contemporary Novelists*) Other novels include *Last Resorts* (1984), *Black Baby* (1988), *Home Rule* (1993) and *Beloved Stranger* (1999), the poignantly familiar story of an elderly man losing his mind and becoming a stranger to his family. From Dublin, Boylan joined the *Irish Press* as a reporter in 1966. Was editor of the magazine, *Image*, and won a Benson and Hedges journalism award in 1974. She has published several excellent short story collections – *A Nail in the Head* (1983), *Concerning Virgins* (1990), *That Bad Woman* (1995). The film, *Making Waves*, nominated for an Oscar in 1988, was based on one of her short stories. A cat-lover, she edited *The Literary Companion to Cats: An Anthology of Prose and Poetry* (1994).

NOEL BROWNE 1915–1997

'My own father died of TB in the early 1950s, and I am painfully aware of the fact that if Noel Browne had arrived on the political scene a few years earlier, the lives of my father and thousands of Irish people could have been saved from this terrible scourge.' The tribute of the late Jim Kemmy, Limerick politician, was typical of those paid to Noel Browne on his death in 1997. He was a man passionately dedicated to the amelioration of unnecessary suffering. Born near Athlone, he experienced great deprivation and suffering in his own family during childhood. The generosity of the Chance family allowed him to study medicine at Trinity College, Dublin. Realising that he could achieve more as a politician than as a doctor, he joined Clann na Poblachta. As Minister for Health he oversaw the virtual eradication of TB. His advocacy of the Mother and Child Scheme was defeated by a combination of the hierarchy and other conservative forces. In the wake of this defeat, he resigned as Minister for Health. He continued as a politician, far too committed to alleviating social injustice ever to settle easily into any particular party. After his retirement he wrote the autobiographical *Against the Tide* (1986).

BILL BRYSON 1951–

'I come from Des Moines. Somebody had to . . .'. Opening lines from *The Lost Continent* exemplify the tone employed by Bryson in his wry examinations of community, places, language and change. He didn't remain there. Visited England as a college student in 1973 and stayed for more than twenty years. Worked for the *Independent* and the *Times*. *The Lost Continent*, his first travel book, was the unflattering account of an American voyage of re-discovery embarked upon in 1987. *A Walk in the Woods* (1997), probably his most popular book, is the much more demanding journey of discovery and self-discovery, in the company of the distressingly overweight Katz, on the 2000 mile Appalachian Trail (they covered less than half). Has written of his travels in continental Europe (*Neither Here nor There*), but is at his best when writing about the US and Britain. *Notes from a Small Island* was televised on ITV in 1999. *I'm a Stranger Here Myself* describes the effect of his return to America and his observations on the changes that have taken place. Books on linguistics include *The Mother Tongue: English and How it Got that Way* (1990) and *Made in America* (1994).

GEORGE CAMPBELL 1917–1979

A painter and stained-glass artist, Campbell, like his friend, Jack Yeats, had 'this extraordinary sense of the archetypal. His Connemara peasants are peasants for all time; his Connemara gypsies, like the gypsies of Andalusia or Malaguena, are eternally wandering.' (Kenneth Jamison, *The Irish Imagination 1959–1971*) Born in Arklow, County Wicklow, he studied in Belfast and Dublin. He was one of the founders of the highly influential Irish Exhibition of Living Art in 1943, 'an unpromising time to launch an annual avant-garde event, but war has often proved a stimulus to creativity . . .'. (Brian Fallon, *An Age of Innocence*) In 1962, he was awarded First Prize in the Open Painting Exhibition, Belfast and was also a prizewinner in an exhibition of Modern Church Art, organised by An Chomhairle Ealaíon. Did much painting in the west of Ireland, but his Spanish paintings are seen as being more passionately inspired – 'sudden climaxes of light and half-light disturb the shadows of narrow streets or flicker to sudden brilliance on the patterned earth colours of a sombre landscape.' (Jamison) A regular exhibitor at the Ritchie Hendriks Gallery (Dublin). Held one-man exhibitions in London, New York, Boston – and several in Galway.

MOYA CANNON 1956–

'You must take a well-cut oar and go on till you reach a people who know nothing of the sea and never use salt with their food, so that our crimson-painted ships and the long oars that serve those ships as wings are quite beyond their ken.' The Odyssey introduces Cannon's first book of poems, *Oar* (first published by Salmon, 1990 and recently reissued by Gallery), which won the Brendan Behan Memorial Prize for a first collection. 'Complicated things happen simply in these poems. The Burren's dove-saints hatch out under the eyes of raptors; old wooden sailboats of Connemara take root in salt water.' (Tim Robinson, Burren map-maker) Cannon studied history and politics at UCD and Corpus Christi College, Cambridge. Has given poetry readings in Ireland, Britain, Germany and Austria, and has published poems in international journals and anthologies. Spent 1994–95 as writer-in-residence at Trent University, Ontario. Has broadcast on RTÉ radio and TV and on BBC Radio 4. Some of her verse has been set to the music of Galway-based composer, Jane O'Leary. Editor of *Poetry Ireland Review*, 1995. Lives in Galway. Her second collection, *The Parchment Boat*, was published in 1997.

CIARÁN CARSON 1948–

The Belfast poet was educated at Queen's University. Was civil servant, teacher and musician before joining the Northern Ireland Arts Council. His collection of poems, *The New Estate* (1976), 'illustrates his minimalist approach to language and imagery.' (*Modern Irish Lives*) Ten years after his first collection of poetry, Carson published *The Irish for No*. Edna Longley hailed it as 'the most innovative book of poems published by an Irishman this year.' Two years later, *Belfast Confetti* won the *Irish Times*/Aer Lingus Irish Literature Prize. *First Language* won the inaugural T.S. Eliot Prize for the best collection of new poetry, 1993. *Opera et Cetera* was Poetry Book Society Choice. Other work includes *The Insular Celts* (1973), while *Last Night's Fun* (1996) reflects his strong interest in Irish traditional music. *The Star Factory* (1997) was described by critic, Tom Adair (*The Irish Times*), as 'an undefinable, indispensable, genre-defying book. Riffle its pages and sense the presence of Carson's dire, redoubtable, doted-on, infamous town and of Carson himself . . .' *Fishing for Amber* (1999), a book of loosely-connected stories, is a 'kaleidoscope of folk tales, mermaids, demons and saints.' (Ian Kilroy, *The Irish Times*).

PHILIP CASEY 1950–

Poet and novelist and playwright. Born in London to Irish parents. Grew up in County Wexford. He published his first collection of poetry, *Those Distant Summers*, in 1980. A second collection, *After Thunder*, came out in 1985. *The Year of the Knife*, published in1991, combined new poems with a 'retrospective' from his two previous books. Michael Hartnett praised *The Year of the Knife* for its 'precision, compassion and images that surpass the common run of language'. His first play, *The Cardinal*, was premiered in Hamburg in 1990. His novel, *The Fabulists*, published in 1994, won the inaugural Kerry Ingredients Book of the Year Award at Listowel Writer's Week. A second novel, *The Water Star*, was published in 1999. 'His first novel *The Fabulists* (1994) won acclaim; his new one affirms that he is a writer with a gift for uncovering the tortuous impulses of his characters with a lucid and affecting eye . . . *The Water Star* is a bittersweet testimony to the never-ending struggle between exile and assimilation.' (John Tague, *Times Literary Supplement*) Casey also maintains an excellent website with biographical details on many Irish writers.

ANNE CHAMBERS 1950–

In her introduction to the revised biography of the sixteenth century pirate queen, *Granuaile*, Chambers (historian, biographer, novelist, scriptwriter) says that 'she has changed my life, leading me on my own voyage of self-discovery, making me abandon one career midstream for the precarious life of a writer, sending me halfway round the world to tell her story from Connemara to Kingston, introducing me to people in every walk of life . . .'. From Castlebar, County Mayo, Chambers graduated from University College, Cork. Worked in the Central Bank. Her works include *Granuaile: The Life and Times of Grace O'Malley* (1979, revised edition, 1998), *Chieftain to Knight: Tibbott-ne-Long Bourke, First Viscount of Mayo* (1983), *Eleanor, Countess of Desmond* (1986), *La Sheridan, Adorable Diva* (1989), and an acclaimed novel, *The Geraldine Conspiracy* (1995), 'a colourful and dashing chronicle'. (*The Irish Times*) Chambers was responsible for design and implementation of the Grace O'Malley Visitor Centre in Louisburgh, County Mayo, and is an honorary member of the O'Malley Clan. Has written a number of documentaries for RTÉ and is currently writing filmscripts, several of which have been optioned internationally and are in the process of being developed.

'All the things I loved were disappearing. The saddest thing for me was the ransacking of the library: the golden tiled roof, the delicately sculpted windows, the blue painted chair . . . Bookshelves were turned upside down, and some pupils tore books to pieces just for the hell of it.' Born in Sichuan Province, China, Jung Chang makes her appearance one third of the way through the deeply moving personal story of one family's terrifying progress through the nightmare of twentieth century Chinese history. A Red Guard briefly at the age of fourteen, she worked as peasant, 'barefoot doctor', steelworker and electrician before becoming an English-language student at Sichuan University. It was there that she heard of Mao's death. 'The news filled me with such euphoria that for an instant I was numb.' Left China for Britain in 1978. First person from People's Republic of China to receive doctorate from a British University. In 1988 she heard the story of her mother's life and that of her grandmother. She decided to write *Wild Swans – Three Daughters of China* (translated into twenty-five languages since its publication in 1991).

He may have been born in County Antrim, but '[h]e's the urban cowboy of broken hearts, and he shoots from the lip.' (Harry Novak) Living 'in exile' in Newcastle, where he is a part-time lecturer and stand-up comic, as well as poet. Edited *The Echo Room*, a poetry magazine, in Newcastle upon Tyne. Bloodaxe has published two collections of his poetry, *The Irish Card* (1993) – 'a tearful and brilliant testament of estrangement and exile.' (Novak) and *Sacrilege* (1998) – '*Sacrilege* finds him in the last chance saloon of inner exile, firing off irreverent messages to anyone who'll listen' (Novak). Cleary is currently focused on a new collection to be called *Stranger in the House*. The theme of this new collection is personal disorder. He is a noted performer of his own works which have been described as 'straight-talking, comic, neurotic, deeply moving'. 'The most exciting reading I've ever been at.' (Bernard Stone, London bookseller, to Tom Kenny) Gave a reading at the Cúirt festival in Galway.

'Intelligent, honest, self-wounding, enraged in general at the demeaned circumstances of an Ireland uniquely catholic, commercial and complaisant, Clifton is the inheritor of Austin Clarke's indigenous obsessions and costive lyricism. There is, however, a distinctive, personal fever and chill about his work.' (*Field Day Anthology*) Clifton, who was born in Dublin, taught English in West Africa for two years. Later worked for the Government in the administration of aid programmes for Indo-Chinese refugees in Thailand. He won the Patrick Kavanagh award in 1981. Irish representative at the Iowa International Writers' Program, and writer-in-residence at the Robert Frost Place, New Hampshire 1986. Work includes *The Walls of Carthage* (1977), *Office of the Salt Merchant* (1979), *Comparative Lives* (1982), *The Liberal Cage* (1988), *Selected Poems, 1973–1988* and *The Desert Route* ('Anyone who has written something of the order of "Monsoon Girl" has to be very good; and so it has proved.' Derek Mahon), *At the Grave of Silone*, and *Night Train through the Brenner*. Has lived in Italy and France. *On the Spine of Italy* (1999) is an account of a year spent with his wife, Deirdre Madden, in an Italian mountain village.

Sir James Comyn (son of James Comyn QC of Clare) was born in Dublin, but educated in England. A member of the English legal profession for many years and Chairman of the Bar Council 1973–74. Among his clients at the English Bar were Lord Lucan, Will Owen, MP, *Times Newspapers* and *Private Eye*. Was a High Court judge (1979-85). Is a member of both the Irish and Hong Kong Bars. As well as writing legal texts, he has written several books of Rumpolesque-like memoirs from his life as a barrister and High Court judge. They are packed with entertaining anecdotes and reflections on legal matters. On the right to silence he has said that 'it may be explicable in certain circumstances . . . many lies are told (or truth withheld) so as not to expose infidelity or to conceal one's movements from wife and family. We must try and strike a fair balance between silence and duty to speak, and in the latter to point out that not all lies are incriminating.' (*Leave to Appeal*) Other books include *Summing it Up*, *Watching Brief*. Co-wrote, with Robert Johnson, *Wills and Intestacies* and *Contract*.

Originally trained as an actor with the Bristol Old Vic Theatre School. From County Cavan, he has written both fictional and autobiographical accounts of his territory. *A Border Station* (1989) is a series of interlinked stories tracing the development of a young boy (son of a guard) as he becomes increasingly aware of the tension within his parent's marriage, and the reality of political and religious divisions which abound in this border county. Connaughton's own father was a sergeant, and he grew up as a guard's son, living on the Cavan-Fermanagh border. His second book, *The Run of the Country,* 1991 (which was filmed) revisits the same ground, this time in novel form. *A Border Diary* (1995) is autobiographical. With Jim Sheridan, he co-wrote the screenplay for *My Left Foot*, Academy Award-winning film of the life of Christy Brown, writer and painter (played by Hugh O'Conor and Daniel Day-Lewis). Also wrote *The Playboys*, with Aidan Quinn and Niamh Cusack. Has recently co-written a screenplay, *The Lord of the Dance*, in collaboration with former *Riverdance* star, Michael Flatley. Won a Hennessy Award for New Irish Writing and a Royal Court Most Promising Playwright Award.

Conroy is a naturalist, artist, broadcaster and much-loved author and illustrator of children's fiction. His books for younger readers include such titles as *The Owl Who Couldn't Give A Hoot*, *The Tiger Who Was A Roaring Success* and *Elephant at the Door* (the teaser asks you to suppose you wished for something very big and pink, like an elephant, and it came true!). For children who like to participate he has devised several activity books – *The Don Conroy Wildlife, Colouring and Activity Book*, *Cartoon Fun* and *Wildlife Fun*. Older children are served by the impressive "Wings" trilogy, *On Silent Wings*, *Sky Wings* and *Wild Wings*, featuring by turn a young barn owl who has to survive alone after his mother's death in a trap, a falcon called upon to overcome evil with the assistance of a magic feather, and a kestrel who must save the world from a colony of evil rats. Other books include *The Vampire Journal*, *The Celestial Child* (short-listed for a Bisto Book of the Year Award) and *Seal of Approval*. He is an original member of *The Den* team on RTÉ Network 2 and children are invited to Draw with Don every week.

Educated at Blackrock College, he joined *The Evening Press* as a copyboy in 1954. Became editor of *The Irish Press* (now defunct) in 1968, one of the youngest editors to be appointed to a national newspaper. A frequent contributor to radio and television at home and abroad. His books include: *Ireland Since the Rising*, *The IRA*, *Ireland – a Personal View*, *On the Blanket*, and the excellent biography, *Michael Collins*. A man with a profound understanding of the complexities of republicanism, he commented in *The Irish Times* (in the wake of the Omagh bombing in 1998) that the 'crossroads which Michael Collins came to when he signed the Treaty inescapably loomed up for Gerry Adams when he signed the Belfast Agreement' but with several advantages denied to Collins, the most important being that there was no 'Machiavellian de Valera beside him deliberately creating a divided Treaty delegation'. He pleaded for the split in the Republican movement, evidenced by the bombing itself, not to be allowed to derail the Belfast Agreement. 'Talking at Stormont is preferable to weeping over graves in Co Tyrone.' He is currently a columnist with *Ireland on Sunday*.

Samuel Beckett: The Last Modernist (1996) was described by Eileen Battersby (*The Irish Times*) as 'one of the best biographies published anywhere of anyone, an atmospheric and international study of one of the century's undisputed originals and a dazzling exploration of an individual formed by one culture, who sought and was absorbed by another.' Cronin was born in County Wexford. Was associate editor of *The Bell* and literary editor of *Time and Tide*. *A Question of Modernity* (1966) established him as an important literary critic, while his memoir of literary life in Dublin in the 1940s and 1950s, *Dead as Doornails* (1976), is described as being 'on a par with those by George Moore and Oliver St John Gogarty which memorialised earlier decades.' (*Field Day Anthology*) Wrote for *The Irish Times* during the 1970s. He is also a fine poet, *R.M.S. Titanic* and his sonnet sequence *The End of the Modern World* being particularly highly regarded. Other publications include *The Life of Riley* (1964), *Collected Poems 1950–73*, *The Life and Times of Flann O'Brien* (1989) and *The Minotaur and Other Poems* (1999). Was cultural adviser to Taoiseach Charles Haughey (1980–83) and oversaw the establishment of Aosdána.

MARGARETTA D'ARCY 1934–

Playwright and social activist. From Dublin, but has lived in Galway for many years. Met playwright, John Arden, while working in the theatre in London. In 1968 became involved in both the civil rights and republican movements. Organised protests against British government's policy in Northern Ireland and was jailed several times for her political activities. *Tell Them Everything* 'is a moving, vivid account of the experiences of D'Arcy's terms in prison.' (Bernard McKenna, *Dictionary of Irish Writers*) She believes strongly in the ability of women to make themselves heard and is a founder member of Women in Media & Entertainment and Radio Pirate-Woman. *Galway's Pirate Women, a Global Trawl* was compiled by D'Arcy and published by Women's Pirate Press in 1996. Many of her plays have been collaborative ventures with her husband, John Arden, staged for and by local communities. Works include *Ars Longa, Vita Brevis* (a children's play), *The Little Grey Home in the West*, *The Non-Stop Connolly Show*, *Vandaleur's Folly* and *Whose Is the Kingdom?* (for BBC radio). As playwrights she and Arden have been admired for 'the ability of their sometimes radical expressions to maintain their dramatic integrity . . .' . (McKenna)

ROALD DAHL 1916–1990

Born in Wales to Norwegian parents. Worked for Shell Oil Company in East Africa. When the Second World War broke out, he joined the RAF. Injured in a plane crash in the Libyan Desert. Sent to Washington as assistant air attaché to the British Embassy. An article he wrote on his flying experiences for *Saturday Evening Post* started him on his writing career. *Kiss Kiss*, a collection of short stories, was published 1960. His short stories have been translated into many languages. His first book for children, *James and the Giant Peach*, was published in 1961. The 1996 film is described in Maltin's *Movie & Video Guide* as '[a] rare movie that creates a world all its own, and an even rarer children's film that has real wit and imagination.' Subsequent children's books include *Charlie and the Chocolate Factory*, *Charlie and the Great Glass Elevator*, *Danny, the Champion of the World* and *Matilda*. Judges described *The Witches* (Whitbread Award, 1983) as 'funny, wise, deliciously disgusting, a *real* book for children. From the first paragraph to the last, we felt we were in the hands of a master.' Recently voted British readers' favourite author in a poll for World Book Day.

ADELE DALSIMER 1939–2000

In 1999, Dalsimer, New York born academic, received an honorary doctorate from the National University of Ireland, for her 'unique and outstanding scholarly contributions to the field of Irish Studies'. Artists, writers, politicians, musicians, academics have all benefited from the Irish Studies programme which resulted from a unique collaboration between a historian and a scholar in the English department at Boston College in the late 1970s. Beginning with a 'team-taught' course, entitled 'The Politics and Literature of Irish Freedom', Adele Dalsimer and Kevin O'Neill built, over two decades, an outstandingly innovative interdisciplinary programme of Irish Studies. Early visitors included Heaney, Muldoon, Fitzgerald, MacBride, Hume and Haughey. Links were forged between Boston College and the National Gallery, the Hugh Lane Gallery and IMMA. The Irish-language poet, Nuala Ní Dhomhnaill, was Burns Visiting Scholar 1998–99. 1999 also saw the fifteenth anniversary of a co-operative programme between Boston College and the Abbey Theatre. Served as board member of both the American Conference for Irish Studies and the International Association for the Study of Irish Literatures. Her books include *The Unappeasable Shadow: Shelley's influence on Yeats* and *Kate O'Brien: A Critical Study*.

ITA DALY 1944–

Daly first came to prominence as a writer of short stories, winning an *Irish Times* short story competition in 1975, and two Hennessy Awards. In 1980, she published a collection of her short stories, *The Lady with Red Shoes*. 'Both stories have privileged narrators recreating in a similar location their apparently intact and secure world. Both, however, write an epitaph for their world when they recount an apparently isolated incident that symbolically brings their world to a close and ushers in a new dispensation.' (*The Field Day Anthology* comparing the title story to William Trevor's 'Beyond the Pale') Born in Drumshambo, County Leitrim. Moved to Dublin in 1957. Graduated in English and Spanish from University College, Dublin. Taught for several years. 'Daly's work for adults is analytic and introspective, delving into the consciousness of mainly solitary protagonists.' (*Modern Irish Lives*) Published her first novel, *Ellen,* in 1986, followed by *A Singular Attraction* (1987), *Dangerous Fictions* (1989), *All Fall Down* (1992) and *Unholy Ghost* (1996). Children's fiction includes *Candy on the DART* (1989), *Candy and Sharon Olé* (1991). Her work appears in German, Danish and Swedish.

'. . . a liberating force in Irish language poetry . . . The jazzy urgency of his style made Gaelic go bebop in the night with a swinging, snazzy self-confidence. For a lot of us who came to poetry in the 70s and 80s he was the tuned-in, amped-up, street-wise cosmopolitan who set the fads, the lingo and the stances. His is an eloquent achievement, a record of richly human poems brought back from the edge of the abyss, from a zone of fear and desperation.' (Cathal Ó Searcaigh, *Watching the River Flow*) Davitt was born in Cork, and did Celtic studies at University College, Cork. Manager of the Slógadh music festival. Editor of the poetry journal *Innti* (1970–). Produced the television documentaries *Joe Heaney: Sing the Dark Away* and *John Montague: Rough Fields*. Won the Butler Literary Award in 1994. Works include *Gleann ar Ghleann* (1982), *Bligeard Sráide* (1983) and *Rogha Dánta 1968–84* (1987). A participant in Turas na bhFilí, an annual cultural exchange between the Irish Gaeltacht and Scotland's Gàidhealtachd. Co-edited *Sruth na Maoile* a tri-lingual anthology of poetry from Ireland and Scotland. Recently published *Freacnairc Mhearcair/The Oomph of Quicksilver: Selected Poems 1970–1998* (2000).

'Dawe's lyrics are like messages from an Ulster protestant sensibility that has decided to go it alone into what is both expected and unexpected in the life of Ireland, north and south.' (*Field Day Anthology*) From Belfast, educated at the New University of Coleraine and University College, Galway, where he taught for several years. Now teaches in Trinity College, Dublin. Was awarded the Macauley Fellowship in Literature for *The Lundys Letter* (1985). Received a Hawthornden International Fellowship in 1987. 'A tolerant and tireless mediator between the Northern and Southern literary communities' (Dennis O'Driscoll, *The Southern Review*). Founded the arts review, *Krino* (1986). Co-edited, with Edna Longley, *Across a Roaring Hill: The Protestant Imagination in Modern Ireland* (1985). His poetry includes *Heritages* (1976), *Sheltering Places* (1978), *The Water Table* (1990), *Sunday School* (1991) and *Heart of Hearts* (1995), praised for its 'balance between the richly inhabited, familial world of the first section and the chaste absences of the second.' (Tom Kilroy) Other publications include *Against Piety: Essays in Irish Poetry* (1995), *The Rest is History: A Critical Memoir* (1998) *The Morning Train* (1999) and *Stray Dogs and Dark Horses* (2000).

Born Limerick and educated in University College, Dublin. Professor of Modern Irish Language and Literature in UCD (1960) and Professor of Irish Dialectology (1978). Editor of English–Irish Dictionary and Consultant Editor of Irish–English Dictionary. General Editor of the Royal Irish Academy's projected Historical Dictionary of Modern Irish (still ongoing). '. . . [P]erhaps his most abiding preoccupation throughout his career was with vocabulary, with words as part of the living working texture of the language and as a vehicle of social discourse and narrative. It was this broader interest that prompted him while Professor of Modern Irish in UCD to establish there a valuable dialect archive, and in due course to publish a selection of the material he had obtained from one of his sources and friends, Tomás Laighléis, of Mionlach, near Galway City.' (Professor Proinsias MacCana) Set up a language laboratory in UCD, the first of its kind in any university in the British Isles, revolutionising the approach to the teaching of modern spoken Irish. Books include *Scothscéalta le Pádraic Ó Conaire*, *Seanchas Thomáis Laighleis*, *The Diary of Humphrey O'Sullivan 1827–1835*. Founder member of Cumann Merriman, which runs annual summer and winter schools.

Poet, editor, translator and critic. Born and educated in Cork. His PhD was a study of Máirtín Ó Cadhain's fiction. Began contributing to the poetry journal *Innti* (which he subsequently edited) in 1980. Spent nine years in Australia working in community and ethnic radio. Part of contemporary renaissance in Irish-language poetry, he has been reluctant to have his poetry translated into English, not through hostility to English, but because he feels that the original needs breathing space if it is not to be rendered invisible by its translation. Has twice won the Seán Ó Ríordáin Prize and became first poet writing in the Irish language to win the O'Shaughnessy Award (2000), a major US literary prize. Has edited *The Cúirt Journal* and *Irish Review*. Works include *Próca Solais is Luatha* (1988), *30 Dán* (1992), *Aimsir Bhreicneach/Freckled Weather* (1993) – published in Australia and short-listed for the Victorian Premier's Award for Literary Translation – *Góbán Cré is Cloch/Sentences of Earth and Shore* (1996), *Seo. Siúd. Agus Uile* (1997) and *Corcach agus Dánta Eile* (1999). Published, with Seán Ó Tuama, a 'rigorous anthology' of twentieth century poetry in Irish, *Coiscéim na hAoise Seo* (1991). Edited Michael Davitt's bilingual collection of poems, *Freacnairc Mhearcair/The Oomph of Quicksilver* (2000).

ANNE DE WINTON 1912–
CATHERINE KENNEDY 1914–2000

Anne, Catherine and Richard were the children of Lady Augusta Gregory's only son, Robert, killed in the last year of the First World War. They spent their childhood in Coole, and in 1970 Anne published *Me and Nu* (her sister's nickname), a recollection of that magical period. Their grandmother, Yeats' friend and colleague, was hostess to all the leading literary figures of the period, and her granddaughter recollects how some of the 'towering' figures appeared to the children. 'Mr Yeats didn't speak much – while we were there anyway – and seemed sunk in thought, miles away, though he never seemed to miss any food. Grandma always seemed to be filling his cup, which he passed up the moment it was empty, without looking up and without a word.' Lady Gregory died in 1932, and the house was subsequently destroyed. For the past six years, Anne and Catherine came to 'The Autumn Gathering' (a weekend of reflection on the life and times of Lady Gregory inaugurated by a group of Galway women) at Coole Park and led groups through the grounds. Catherine, the younger of the two sisters, died earlier this year.

JOHN F. DEANE 1943–

A poet himself, he is also a publisher and accomplished translator. Founded Dedalus Press which publishes Irish poets, as well as bilingual editions of contemporary European poets. These include Deane's own translations from the Swedish of Tomas Traströmer, *The Wild Marketplace*, and from the Romanian of Marin Sorescu, *The Youth of Don Quixote*. In 1978 he founded Poetry Ireland. From Achill Island, Deane graduated from University College, Dublin. Has written several collections of poetry including *High Sacrifice*, *Road with Cypress and Star*, *Far Country*, *The Stylized City:New and Selected Poems* and *Christ, with Urban Fox*. Many of his poems are meditations on the meaning of spirituality. Gives poetry readings throughout Europe and the US and his poems have been translated into several languages. Elected secretary general of the European Academy of Poetry, 1996. In 1998 was awarded the O'Shaughnessy Prize for Poetry. In 1994, he published his first collection of short stories, and a novel, *One Man's Place*. More novels followed: *Flightlines* (1996) and *In the Name of the Wolf* (1999) – a gothic tale, '[c]lipping along at a ferocious pace . . . convincingly unreal stuff.' (John Kenny, *The Irish Times*) *The Coffin Master and Other Stories* appeared earlier this year.

GERTRUDE DEGENHARDT 1940–

'What is so special about Gertrude Degenhardt's women? They make music; they play; they dance . . . they are acrobatic . . . I have one at home who plays a drum which is on the back of her neck with her heels!' (Tom Kenny opening an exhibition of the artist's paintings in Dublin) And then there are the men – in *Farewell to Connaught*, a portfolio of dry point etchings, wind pervades everything. Music is the wind that lifts angular men from their barstools to dance with wild fury on their pointed feet. Etched directly onto copperplate, on location, 'the furrows and scratches in the copperplate must be invertedly visualized as printed on paper . . . A welcome side-effect advenes: the expectant curiosity of those perceiving that they are being observed and drawn is by no means satisfied because they are unable to recognize themselves in the copperplate . . . Instantly, they turn away, and their suspense dissolving, they become their old selves again . . .' . (Hans Peter Willberg) Born in New York, but raised in West Berlin. Lives in Germany. First came to Ireland twenty-five years ago, to illustrate a German language edition of Liam O'Flaherty's short stories. Has been coming ever since.

FRANK DELANEY 1942–

Frank Delaney is widely known as a broadcaster on British radio and television (particularly BBC2 and Sky TV). He is also a popular novelist. *My Dark Rosaleen* (1988), his first novel, was very successful. Other titles followed – *The Sins of the Mothers*, *The Amethysts*, 'an exotic offering which, read in a leisurely way, will not induce our hero's malady, Montezuma's Revenge, but rather a feeling of well-being and a pleasant aftertaste' (Vincent Banville, *The Irish Times*) and *Desire and Pursuit*, 'Delaney has an unfailing grip on his material, and this is a quality page-turner – moving, compelling, satisfying.' (Arminta Wallace, *The Irish Times*) Delaney grew up in Tipperary, worked first as a banker, but joined RTÉ in the early 1970s. Presented his award-winning programme *Bookshelf* on BBC Radio 4 for five years and was a member of the Booker Prize selection committee 1982. *James Joyce's Odyssey: A Guide to the Dublin of Ulysses* (1981) is a guide not only to the Dublin of Ulysses but to Ulysses itself. Other works include *Betjeman Country* (1983), *A Walk to the Western Isles: After Boswell and Johnson* (1993) and *A Walk in the Dark Ages*.

'Cool and candid at the same time, Greg Delanty's poems move at a quick pace and at an equal distance from the sentimental and the skilful. His innocent pitch of voice, which was there from the start, has been maintained and developed through his subsequent absorption of the open styles of American Poetry.' (*Field Day Anthology*) Delanty was born in Cork and went to University College, Cork. Won a Patrick Kavanagh Award 1983. This was followed by an Alan Dowling Poetry Fellowship in the United States in 1986. Poet-in-residence in Franconia, New Hampshire, 1988. Took second place in the British Poetry Society's National Poetry competition in 1999. Lives and teaches in the United States. *Southward* (1992) is described as containing '. . . poems that brilliantly balance strict, formal control with vivid and rich language. The result is a rare thing: an expatriate's account of his native land that is not only a pleasure to read, but completely believable to boot.' (*Harvard Review*) Other works include *Cast in the Fire* (1986), *American Wake* (1995) and *The Hell Box* (1998). Co-edited, with Nuala Ní Dhomhnaill, *Jumping off Shadows: Selected Contemporary Irish Poetry.*

'For a long time Don DeLillo has been tracking America, its paranoia, its vulnerabilities, its hysteria, its images, its shaky icons, its very existence, with an epic intensity equalled only by William Gaddis and Thomas Pynchon . . . With the publication of *Mao II* in 1991, DeLillo seemed not only to be challenging mass culture and America's sense of self, but the relevance of language in a world in which the word has been supplanted by the visual image.' (Eileen Battersby, *The Irish Times*) The author of such books as *The Names* (his masterpiece, in Battersby's view), *Libra* (a compelling look at the personal and possible inner world of Lee Oswald) and *White Noise* was born in New York City and educated at Fordham University, Bronx, New York. *Underworld*, first published in 1997, is Cold War America reaching into the reader's head like an echo that never disappears. 'He offers us another history of ourselves, the unofficial underground moments.' (Michael Ondaatje) He has won the National Book Award, the PEN/Faulkner Award for Fiction, and the Irish Times/Aer Lingus International Fiction Prize in 1989 with *Libra*.

Best known in County Galway (where he has lived since the early 1970s) as author of *Le Taxi Mauve*, a story of expatriates in Ireland, subsequently filmed as 'The Purple Taxi' starring, amongst others, Charlotte Rampling, Peter Ustinov and Fred Astaire. A prolific novelist, *Les Poneys Sauvages* (1970), *Le jeune homme vert* (1975) and *Les Vingt Ans du Jeune Homme Vert* (1977) are the works with which English readers are most familiar. Born in Paris, he began to work for the publication *L'Action Française* during the war. After the war he travelled extensively in Germany, Switzerland, Italy and Africa. His first novel, *Je ne veux jamais l'oublier*, published in 1950, linked him to the new right-wing movement in French literature. Awarded a Rockefeller Foundation bursary in 1951, he spent time in the US where he studied American theatre. Since the late 1950s, Déon has lived largely outside France – in Portugal, on the Greek island of Spetsai and, finally, in East Galway. He is a member of the Academie Française. Other works include *La Corrida* (1952), *Le Dieu Pale* (1954), *Les Trompeuses Espérances* (1956), *Les Gens de la Nuit* (1958). *Jeu de Miroirs* was published in 1998.

A successful writer for both children and adults, best known for her novel, *Across the Bitter Sea* (1973). Born in Galway, her father was Professor of Chemistry in University College, Galway. Her uncle, Joseph Plunkett, was executed in 1916. Her first husband, Cormac Ó Cuilleanáin, was professor of Irish at University College, Cork. Eiléan Ní Cuilleanáin, the poet, is their daughter. Cormac Ó Cuilleanáin died in 1970. In 1974 she married the academic, Vivian Mercier, and they divided their time between the US and Ireland. Between 1950 and 1970, Dillon had a book published in every year but 1951. She continued to write up to the time of her death, her last task being the editing of Vivian Mercier's posthumously published book, *Modern Irish Literature: Sources and Founders*. She wrote in both Irish and English. *The Lost Island* (1952) and *The Singing Cave* (1959) are the best known of her children's fiction. *The Island of Ghosts* won the Bisto Book of the Year Award in 1990. Her final children's work was *Children of Bach* (1993). She also wrote plays and screenplays. Lectured in creative writing in Trinity College, Dublin (1971–72). Writer in residence, University College, Dublin (1988).

J.P. DONLEAVY 1926–

The author of *The Ginger Man* (first published in France in 1955, not appearing in Britain until 1963) currently lives the life of a squire in a spacious eighteenth-century house in Mullingar where he farms the estate. Born in New York, he came to Dublin on a GI grant after the Second World War. *The Ginger Man*, a banned cause célèbre – 'a magistrate in Manchester made an order for the book's destruction' (Donleavy to Róisín Ingle, *The Irish Times*), is set in Trinity, where Donleavy took his degree. John Ryan's (proprietor of Bailey's bar and restaurant, editor of *Envoy*) 'milieu embraced the famous Catacombs, the curious set of people described in J.P. Donleavy's novel, *The Ginger Man* . . .'. (Brian Fallon, *An Age of Innocence*) Also a play, *The Ginger Man* (originally forced to close in Dublin) was performed there as recently as last summer. Other works include the novels *A Singular Man, The Saddest Summer of Samuel S, The Beastly Beatitudes of Balthazar B*, and, most recently, *The Woman who Liked Clean Restrooms*. His play, *Fairy Tales of New York*, won *Evening Standard* 'Most Promising Playwright of the Year' Award in 1960.

KATIE DONOVAN 1962–

'Central to her subversive, subtle work is a contrasting tension of extremes honed by disarming candour, detachment, intense emotion and violent, savage imagery. The symbol of the goddess which dominates several of the poems is both alll-powerful and vulnerable, usually personified as the Celtic horse deity, Epona.' (Eileen Battersby, *The Irish Times*, on Donovan's second collection of poetry, *Entering the Mare*, published 1997). Talking about the perceived eroticism in her poetry she points out the consistent denial of female sexuality – 'There's such a coldness about the way fertility is presented. The Virgin Mary is, what? A woman in a blue dress who has been denied a body and normal human emotions.' (Donovan to Battersby) Poet, *Irish Times* journalist and critic, Donovan wrote an interesting analysis of the increasingly confident Irish female poetic voice for the special summer (1995) edition of *Southern Review*. Her father is Irish, her mother is Canadian. She spent her early childhood in County Wexford. Graduated from Trinity College, Dublin. First collection, *Watermelon Man*, was published in 1993. Co-edited, with Brendan Kennelly and A. Norman Jeffares, *Ireland's Women: Writings Past and Present*.

THEO DORGAN 1953–

Dorgan was born and educated in Cork. Completed an MA in English at University College, Cork and taught there while literature officer at the Triskel Arts Centre. Poetry collections include *Slow Air* (1975), *A Moscow Quartet* (1989), *The Ordinary House of Love* (1990), *Rosa Mundi* (1995) – 'The Match Down the Park' being described as a 'tour de force of a poem recounting the excitement and fervour of a hurling match . . .' (*Waterstone's Guide to Irish Books*) – and *Sappho's Daughter* (1998). He and Máirín Ní Dhonnchadha edited *Revising the Rising* (1991) to provide, in the year of the seventy-fifth anniversary of the Rising, 'a range of opinions on 1916, and its meanings' and 'to bring some civility and calm to what can be a turbulent and sometimes factional debate'. Edited a collection of essays, *Irish Poetry since Kavanagh* (1995), and was co-editor, with Gene Lambert, of *The Great Book of Ireland* (1991). Most recently co-edited, with Noel Duffy, *Watching the River Flow: A Century in Irish Poetry* (1999). Presenter of several book programmes on radio and TV. He is director of *Poetry Ireland* and is acknowledged in *Contemporary Irish Literature* as having done 'great service compiling and editing books on contemporary poetry'.

SEÁN DUNNE 1956–1995

The poet, journalist and broadcaster, Seán Dunne, was born in Waterford. Graduated from University College, Cork. Literary editor of the *Cork Examiner*. He was a broadcaster and contributed regularly to *Sunday Miscellany* and *Poetry Choice* on Radio Éireann. *In My Father's House* (1991) was a sensitive and spiritual account of his childhood in Waterford. He published three poetry collections – *Against the Storm* (1985), *The Sheltered Nest* (1992) and his final collection, *Time and the Island*, which was given to The Gallery Press two weeks before his death. 'A strong musicality and sense of form are inherent in his poems. The domestic life, its dangers, rewards and fragility forms his most prevalent subject matter. His later work displayed a dedication to metaphor and an almost Japanese-like sensitivity to the image.' (*Waterstone's Guide to Irish Books*). He edited *The Cork Anthology* (1993). He also edited *Poets of Munster: An Anthology* (1985) and *An Introduction to Irish Poetry* (1992). His books on spirituality included *The Road to Silence* (1994) and *Something Understood: A Spiritual Anthology* (1995). *The College: A Photographic History of University College, Cork* appeared in 1995.

PAUL DURCAN 1944–

'Durcan's verse is populated by the unlikely and the impossible, from pre-Raphaelite beauties lifted from their canvases and imaginatively transported to the realm of L.A. biker gangs . . . to dancing naked security guards in Bewley's Oriental Café . . .'. (*Contemporary Irish Literature*) But he also 'excels at conveying' tradition to a 'thoroughly modern readership'. Born in Dublin but spent much of his childhood in County Mayo. After a period in England, returned to Ireland and took a degree in archaeology and medieval history at University College, Cork. Received a Patrick Kavanagh award 1974, and his collection *Daddy, Daddy* won the Whitbread prize in 1990. Other works include *O Westport in the Light of Asia Minor* (1974), *Jesus, Break his Fall* (1980), *The Berlin Wall Café* (1985), *Going Home to Russia* (1987), *Crazy About Women* (1991), *New and Selected Poems* (1993). 'Durcan writes long Whitmanesque lines that scout the borders of prose . . . Yet, for all their air of relaxation, the best of them grow in tension as the poet seeks out the desired image or final phrase to which the poem was designed to give birth' (*Field Day Anthology*). *Greetings to our Friends in Brazil* was published last year.

RICHARD ELLMAN 1918–1987

Born in Detroit, Michigan. Graduated from Yale 1941. Served in the US Navy and the Office of Strategic Services. After demobilisation he went to Trinity College, Dublin. '. . . the first sight of Mrs Yeats's study, which had been her husband's, was astonishing . . . Among the scraps were all Yeats's letters to Lady Gregory, done up in innumerable small bundles according to year, with ribbons to hold them together.' (*Yeats: The Man and the Masks*, 1948) A critical study, *The Identity of Yeats*, was published in 1954. Assistant Professor at Harvard University (1948–51). Professor at North Western University, Illinois (1951–68). His biography of James Joyce ('The greatest literary biography of the century', Anthony Burgess) was published in 1959 and won the National Book Award. A revised edition – 'The additions may help to assuage some of the curiosity that still persists about this bizarre and wonderful creature who turned literature and language on end . . .' – won both the Duff Cooper Memorial Prize and the James Tait Black Prize in 1983. Professor of English Literature at Oxford (1970–84). His biography of Oscar Wilde was completed shortly before his death and published posthumously.

EMYR ESTYN EVANS 1905–1989

'I see us riddled with romantic nationalist myths, and fundamentalist loyalist myths, and both are very dangerous . . . because they are both inaccurate and emotive and I don't know what we are going to do about that except hunt for the truth and plead for reason. I've always felt Irish history to be one-sided because we haven't looked enough to the land itself.' (Estyn Evans, quoted in *The Irish Times*) Historians noted his concerns. 'It is not long since Professor Estyn Evans . . . castigated Irish historians *en masse* for their neglect . . . of the physical environment within which our past has been lived.' (F.S.L. Lyons, *Field Day Anthology*) The geographer and anthropologist was born in Wales. Graduated from the University of Wales, Aberysthwyth, where he was inspired by H.J. Fleure. Joined Queen's University, Belfast in 1928 where he remained until his retirement. Became director of the Institute of Irish Studies in 1968. Chairman of the Northern Ireland Committee on Itinerants. Works include *Irish Heritage* (1942), *Mourne Country* (1951), *Irish Folk Ways* (1957), *Prehistoric and Early Christian Ireland* (1966) and *The Personality of Ireland* (1973).

PETER FALLON 1951–

Talking of his double role as publisher and poet to Louise East, *The Irish Times*, Fallon admitted that '[s]ometimes I may have exhausted the energies that might have been put into my own work. That is a price I may have paid.' Born in West Germany, but brought up on a farm in County Meath. Graduated from Trinity College, Dublin. Still lives on a small sheep farm in Meath. Founded the Gallery Press when he was eighteen because he saw a dirth of publishers prepared to publish young Irish poets. Has been a major publisher of Irish literature ever since. Co-edited *The Penguin Book of Contemporary Irish Poetry* (1990) with Derek Mahon. His poetry is rooted in the local. Discussing Fallon's development as a poet, Bernard O'Donoghue (*Contemporary Poets*) commented that 'his first collection tried too hard to draw the universal moral from the stories in his world and consequently seemed too narrow an expression of the poet's view; his later work is much simpler and never forces the moral, with the result that an air of universality is there to be inferred.' Published a selection of old and new poems, *News of the World*, in 1998.

Farrell's first play, *I Do Not Like Thee, Dr. Fell* (1979) is his best known. When it was suggested that he might have come to resent it, the playwright demurred. 'Not at all, I'll always be grateful to it. It's my Catch-22.' (Eileen Battersby, *The Irish Times*) Following that success he left his job with Sealink. Success has continued. Reviewing *Kevin's Bed* (1998), David Nowlan, *The Irish Times,* said, 'In the hands of Alan Ayckbourn . . . there would have been cruel farce. But here everything is softened by compassion and affection which blunts the theatrical impact yet leaves more to remember of the characters who people the play.' In 1999, the Red Kettle Theatre Company revived *Happy Birthday, Dear Alice.* Actress, Anna Manahan (the mother who resists her children's plans to put her in a home), captured the reason for Farrell's popularity. 'We got an extraordinary audience reaction . . . Everyone thinks about their own parents. One woman told me that she saw it twice: the first time, she was shattered, then she watched it again and forgave herself. It's a comedy, with dark undertones.' (Helen Meany, *The Irish Times*) In Farrell's plays, the audience knows the people on the stage. They are themselves.

'In raw poems and atavistic images, Padraic Fiacc has described the sufferings of Northern nationalists'. (Declan Kiberd, *Field Day Anthology*) Fiacc (born Patrick Joseph O'Connor), emigrated to America with his family from Belfast as a young child. He attended St. Joseph's Seminary, Yonkers, New York. Returned permanently to Belfast in 1946. Won the AE Memorial Award in 1947. 'Fiacc's style can be so stark as to make other poets seem artful even at their most plain-spoken . . . an important presence for younger Ulster poets, Fiacc is at his best recording the off-camera moments, the out-takes, of the Ulster conflict . . .' . (Dennis O'Driscoll, *The Southern Review*) Works include *By the Black Stream* (1969), *Odour of Blood* (1973), *Nights in the Bad Place* (1977) and *Ruined pages: Selected Poems of Padraic Fiacc* (1994). In 1974 he edited *The Wearing of the Black*, an anthology which 'remains of relevance as an early act of Ulster stocktaking' (O'Driscoll). Reviewing his latest collection, *Semper Vacare*, Gerald Dawe (*The Irish Times*), said that 'Fiacc's earliest "Celtic Twilight" poems were, even then, shot through with the shocking understanding that life is a kind of ludicrous ordeal.'

'Fitzmaurice is deeply committed to his native place and its poetic traditions, as his own verse – written in English and Irish – makes hauntingly clear.' (*Modern Irish Lives*) That native place is Moyvane, County Kerry where he was born and educated and where he has taught as a national schoolteacher since 1972. A driving force behind Listowel Writers' Week and also a fine musician. Broadcasts regularly on RTÉ radio and television. Awarded a Gerard Manley Hopkins Centenary poetry prize (1989). A prolific poet, he is also a dedicated editor. *Irish Poetry Now: Other Voices* is 'an anthology of poetry not generally available in the anthologies of the literary Establishment . . . drawn from the two languages on this island.' (Fitzmaurice) Edited, with Declan Kiberd, *An Crann Faoi Blath/ The Flowering Tree: Contemporary Irish Poetry with Verse Translations* (1991). Works include *The Space Between* (1993), *Nach Iontach mar atá Rainn do Pháistí* (1994) and *The Village Sings: Poems* (1996). Edited *An Bealach 'na Bhaile, Rogha Dánta, Homecoming* by Cathal Ó Searcaigh, *Kerry through its Writers* (1993) and *The Listowel Literary Phenomenon: North Kerry Writers, A Critical Introduction* (1994). Recently published *Kerry on my Mind: Of Poets, Pedagogues and Place* (1999).

An artist who has held many one-man shows in Kenny's Art Gallery. He is from the Dingle Peninsula in Kerry and in 1989 he returned there to open his own Brandon Gallery. 'All of his inspiration comes from within a stone's throw of his home in Cloghane.' (Tom Kenny) He paints in a heavy impasto style, using strong colours and a simplified canvas. He celebrates bog, sea, skies, the dripping fuschia flowers. He didn't begin to paint seriously until after he had completed a BA in University College, Cork. Trained in Cork and Sligo. One of his most interesting early works was a scroll, thirty yards long, on which he had painted every day for six months – an artist's personal diary. It was shown in Dublin, New York, San Francisco and Canberra. Exhibition venues for his work include Kilcock Art Gallery, the Royal Hibernian Academy, Ireland House, New York, and the Ulster Academy and his work is represented in many public and private collections, including Merrill Lynch Corporate Finance, the AIB Group, Government Buildings, Avonmore PLC, the ESB, Dublin City University, DAIWA Bank PLC, New York, New York University and the Commerz Bank of Frankfurt.

Flanagan was born in Kilfenora, County Clare and went to the local National School from which he passed his leaving certificate 'at about age 14 years'. He became interested in the heritage of his area in the 1930s and spent much time on winter evenings discussing local history with his neighbours (in particular Robert Blake Forster of Ballykeal House). 'Looking back we had a school of history.' During the Second World War he worked in the phosphate mines in North Clare. He moved to Dublin and worked on the buildings. Subsequently he spent twenty-five years in London with the Kodak Company. During all those years, he built up a scrapbook full of articles and photographs and memorabilia of Kilfenora. On his return home, he became a member of the North Clare Historical Society and was persuaded to publish his history of Kilfenora. Copies of *Kilfenora: A History* have been sold around the world. Recently a much-enlarged second edition was published. This guardian of local history lives at Dough, Lahinch, County Clare.

'*The End of the Hunt* (1994) covers the Irish rebellion and civil war, 1919-1923, but with a quicker pace . . . No longer do the characters await history to engulf them: they devour it before it eats them. Possibly Flanagan's greatest achievement is to have captured the zeitgeist of 1798, 1867–1892, and 1919–1921.' Owen Dudley Edwards (*Dictionary of Irish Literature*) is writing about Flanagan's great trilogy of historical novels, *The Year of the French* (televised as a joint French-Irish production), *The Tenants of Time* and *The End of the Hunt*. An academic before he was a novelist, Flanagan's early dissertation, *The Irish Novelists 1800–1850* (1959) was a recognition of complexity, involving 'a study of five islands, for each writer [Maria Edgeworth, Lady Morgan, John Banin, Gerald Griffin and William Carleton] had his own intense understanding of the country which he had taken as his subject.' (Flanagan) Born in Connecticut to a family with roots in Fermanagh. Spent eighteen years as associate professor at the University of California before moving to the State University of New York. Brought out an edition of John Mitchel's *Jail Journal* (1982). A frequent visitor to Ireland since the early 1960s.

The Sportswriter and PEN/Faulkner, Pulitzer Prize-winning sequel, *Independence Day*, both set in New Jersey, were described by novelist and literary critic, John Banville, as 'modern masterpieces'. Ford, the first writer to win both awards for a single work, had not intended to write a sequel, 'but I spent a year, in essence, thinking about the things that would go into this book and finally at the end, I kept finding that all of my notes and all the things I was thinking about were in Frank's voice, and I liked that voice because I thought he was a good sort of negotiator of, of ethical issues, and I thought he was humorous. I thought, you know, I guess I thought he was a good man.' (Richard Ford to Elizabeth Farnsworth of PBS's Newshour) Banville went on to claim 'Occidentals', one of three extended short stories in *Women with Men: Three Stories* (1997) as 'one of the three finest American short stories since the war' (*The Irish Times*). Ford was born in Jackson, Missouri. Has taught at several US colleges and universities. Other works include *The Ultimate Good Luck* (1981) and *A Piece of my Heart* (1987).

'I decided, in January 1970 with little hope of any success, to try my hand at a single, one-off novel, for no better motive than that I happened to be broke and without many prospects after twelve years in journalism. I dashed off *The Day of the Jackal* in thirty-five days, virtually without notes, relying on my memory and keeping the plot in my head . . .'. (Forsyth, introducing a four-novel omnibus comprising *The Day of the Jackal*, *The Odessa File*, *The Dogs of War* and *The Devil's Alternative*) His work as a journalist included a stint with Reuters, and he also worked as correspondent for the BBC. *The Biafra Story* (1969) was a history of the Biafran war. '. . . By the summer of 1973, I had written three novels within forty months, and was extremely tired. With my contract honoured, I decided to call it a day . . .'. *The Devil's Alternative* (1979), *The Fourth Protocol* (1984), *The Negotiator* (1989), *The Fist of God* (1994), and *Icon* (1996) followed that decision. Both *The Day of the Jackal* (starring Cyril Cusack, amongst others) and *The Fourth Protocol* were successfully filmed.

BRIAN FRIEL 1929–

One of Ireland's foremost playwrights, Friel was born in County Tyrone. He taught throughout the 1950s, but has written full-time since then. For Friel, says Christopher Murray (*Contemporary Dramatists*), 'there was an unacknowledged gap between the individual mind (and experience) and a social reality which was crumbling at an alarming rate'. His play, *Philadelphia Here I Come*, starkly shows the disturbance caused by this rift in the character of Gar, whose public utterances and private thoughts are played by two actors who appear simultaneously on the stage. We see Gar emigrating, painfully, not only from Ireland itself, but also from the older countries of his mind. Significantly, as Murray points out, the play (one of the first of the Irish hits on Broadway, in 1966) was originally staged, not at the Abbey, venue for his earlier play, *The Enemy Within*, but at the Gate. The theatre which had rejected Keane and Murphy was out of touch with the seething changing Ireland. Friel was the founder, with the actor, Stephen Rea, of the Field Day Theatre Company in 1980. Some of his best-known plays are *Faith Healer*, *Translations*, and *Dancing at Lugnasa*, recently made into a film.

BRENDAN FULLAM

'I can still hear that voice: "Bail ó Dhia oraibh go léir, a chairde, agus fáilte romhaibh," welcoming, enthusiastic and dramatic, ringing and echoing in my ears. It will always be there, for it was stored computer-like in my very young and impressionable years . . .'. (Fullam in *Legends of the Ash* on Mícheál O'Hehir) The voice was one element which served to deepen Fullam's passionate interest in hurling. Becoming a bank manager did not deflect this interest in any way and frequent moves made during the course of his banking career allowed him to play the game with local teams in several counties. His three books, *Giants of the Ash*, *Hurling Giants* and *Legends of the Ash*, present a series of in-depth interviews with such great hurling heroes of the century as Christy Ring, Peter Cregan, John and Michael Maher, the Rackards and John T. Power (born in 1883, a year before the GAA was founded and in his ninety-ninth year at the time of the interview). Camogie players also feature, most notably Kathleen Mills, Una O'Connor and Marian McCarthy. Fullam himself described the game of hurling as 'truly unique: an "unpremeditated art"'.

PATRICK GALVIN 1927–

'Galvin's unique contribution to Irish poetry is that character-filled surrealism, and a teeming life of working-class Cork, a life that sings and screams with the energy of Behan and Lorca.' (Thomas McCarthy, *Contemporary Poets*) Left school early. Served with the RAF during the war (having joined as an under-age sixteen year old). Began writing poetry around 1950. War correspondent in Korea during the 1950s. Ballad singer in England and the US. Made several records. Best known as a poet, works include *Heart of Grace*, *Christ in London*, *The Woodburners*. Best known poem is 'The Madwoman of Cork'. As well as poetry, he has written several plays, including *And Him Stretched*, *Nightfall to Belfast* and *We do it for Love*. Spent twelve years in Belfast and was resident dramatist at the Lyric Theatre, 1974–77. Has written three autobiographical works, *Song for a Poor Boy*, *Song for a Raggy Boy*. *Song for a Fly Boy* brings him up to the age of eighteen. Says it will be his last. 'because . . . at least in terms of autobiographical material, it's been all downhill since then.' (to *The Irish Times*)

ALLEN GINSBERG 1926–1997

Born in Newark, New Jersey. At Columbia University he met up with Jack Kerouac (*On The Road*) and William S. Burroughs (*The Naked Lunch*) and became immersed in the drugs 'n sex culture. After a brief period as a market researcher, he moved to San Francisco where he published *Howl and Other Poems* (1956), the title poem of which condemned the existing bourgeois culture and proposed a radical and celebratory counter-culture. It became the symbol of the Beat Movement. The title poem of *Kaddish and Other Poems* is a lament for his mother who went insane at a tragically young age and who was institutionalised for much of her adult life. As an enormously popular Beat poet, he was involved in most of the left-wing political movements of the 1960s. Developed a deep interest in Buddhism which is reflected in his later poetry. Although he travelled a great deal, his base, for most of his adult life, was New York City's Lower East Side. Other works include *The Fall of America: Poems of These States, 1965–1971*, which won the National Book Award, *Mind Breaths: Poems 1972–1977*, and *White Shroud: Poems 1980–1985*.

MICHAEL GORMAN 1952–

Gorman was born in Sligo and educated at Summerhill College. He has undertaken such diverse occupations as editing 'Writing in the West' for *The Connacht Tribune*, tutoring in English at NUI, Galway and working as a civil servant with the D.H.S.S in Soho and Westminster. He was also community playwright with Annex Theatre Company. In 1980, the Galway Arts Group published his first collection of poems, *Postcards from Galway*, with illustrations by Joachim Boske. *Waiting for the Sky to Fall* (1984) was followed by *Up She Flew* (1991), published by Salmon Publishing. His poems have appeared in many publications, including *Criterion*, *The Honest Ulsterman*, *The Irish Times*, *Krino*, *Paris Atlantic*, *Quarto* and *The Sunday Tribune*. They have also been read on RTÉ. Brendan Kennelly has described his poems as 'contained, even deliberately subdued', while Eavan Boland called him a 'socially-committed writer who uses narrative to widen the poetic subject'.

GERALD HANLEY 1916–1992

Both Gerald and his possibly more interesting older brother, James (1901–1985), were successful writers. The younger Hanley was born in Cork but lived abroad for much of his life. Joined the British army when war broke out. Served in Burma. Before the war he had worked in East Africa. After the war, he went to Kenya. *The Consul at Sunset* (1951) and *The Year of the Lion* (1959), his most popular novels, are set in the dying empire. Hemingway 'admired his accomplishment in combining action and conscience.' (*Dictionary of Irish Biography*) In *Without Love* (1957), the protagonist, Michael Brennan (serving an international organisation in Barcelona), is forced to examine the irreconcilable conflict between abhorrent actions undertaken for some perceived greater good. Ordered by his superiors to kill a renegade he is 'confronted with the fact that a man by trying to save the world may lose his own soul.' He wrote several other novels and eventually returned to Ireland in the 1980s.

EAMONN GRENNAN 1941–

Poet and translator, ' . . . a true Seer, somebody who reveals the world anew. Reading his poems, we become more eye, more ear, more conscious of the momentousness of the ordinary.' (Cathal Ó Searcaigh, *Watching the River Flow*) Grennan was born in Dublin and educated at University College, Dublin and Harvard. He lived in Italy for a time. Recipient of a fellowship from the National Endowment for the Arts, and a Guggenheim fellowship. Has been writer-in-residence at UCD. He has also taught at the City University of New York. Grennan's critical studies range from Shakespeare and Spenser to the modern poets. 'Not the least remarkable thing about *Wildly for Days* is the sight of such a sophisticated intelligence achieving such an elevated naïveté.' (Derek Mahon) Other works include *What Light There Is* (1987), *As If It Matters* (1991) and *So It Goes* (1995). He has translated *Selected Poems of Giacomo Leopardi* (1995). He teaches at Vassar College and divides his time between the USA and Ireland.

EOGHAN HARRIS 1943–

'The Pope's visit, said Eoghan Harris at the time, would set Ireland back sociologically ten years for about three weeks.' (Nell McCafferty, *Goodnight Sisters*) Harris has always been an astute political commentator. Was a producer with RTÉ from 1966 to 1990, during which period he produced *The Greening of America* (Jacobs Award), and *Darkness Visible* (Silver Bear Award, Berlin). Was an advisor to the Workers Party during the same period, and contributed to several pamphlets, including *Irish Industrial Revolution* (1976), *Land for the People* (1978) and *Television and Terrorism* (1987). In 1990 he acted as campaign strategist in Mary Robinson's successful bid for the presidency. Author of three plays, the best-known of which is *Souper Sullivan*, a famine play in which unskilled labourers convert to the Protestant church in return for soup. It was produced by the Abbey in 1985. Before the production, Harris 'told of Ronald Reagan's visit to Cork [Harris's home city] when graffiti proclaimed the Protestant president a "Souper" because of his conversion from Catholicism.' (Bernard McKenna, *Dictionary of Irish Literature*) Has described the potential of the Belfast Agreement as 'profoundly redemptive'. (*The Irish Times*, October 1999)

TONY HARRISON 1937–

'Behind one image . . . there will always be an incongruous counter-image . . . that will play off the first, that will complicate it or make it a paradox.' (Carol Rutter, editor of *Permanently Bard: Selected Poetry*, 1995) Born in Leeds and won a scholarship to Leeds Grammar School. Read classics and linguistics at Leeds University. Taught in Nigeria and in Prague during the 1960s. Has used the different strands of his background to achieve a unique voice – it 'wants to be accessible, and even at its most inward or confessional it is dramatic and theatrical'. (Rutter) Best known as a theatre and film poet, he has written for the National Theatre, the New York Metropolitan Opera, the BBC and Channel 4. His film poems include *The Blasphemer's Banquet* (his defence of Salman Rushdie) and *The Gaze of the Gorgon* (winner of the Whitbread Poetry Award). *Black Daisies for the Bride* won the Prix Italia in 1994. *The Shadow of Hiroshima* was screened on Channel 4 in 1995 to mark the anniversary of the bombing. Amongst his plays are *The Trackers of Oxyrhynchus*, first performed in Delphi, and *The Prince's Play*.

FRANCIS HARVEY 1925–

The 1980s 'gave us the taut and elegant poems of Frank Harvey, a sadly neglected poet. Elegiac and lyric, regional and specific, true to their own world, they also open out wholeheartedly to other worlds . . . they vibrate in the memory with a profoundly mantric quality.' (Cathal Ó Searcaigh, *Watching the River Flow*) Though born in Enniskillen, for most of his life Francis Harvey has lived in County Donegal. He began as a playwright, winning an RTÉ radio play competition in 1958. *They Feed Christians to Lions Here, Don't They?* won an O.Z. Whitehead award and was performed both in the Peacock Theatre in Dublin and in America. His radio plays have been broadcast by RTÉ, the BBC and in several European countries. In more recent years, he has turned to poetry. In 1977, he won *The Irish Times*/Yeats International Summer School Poetry Competition and The Gallery Press published his first collection, *In the Light on the Stones*, the following year. *The Rainmakers* was published in 1988 and more recently Dedalus published *The Boa Island Janus*.

MICHAEL HARTNETT 1941–1999

'I belong to the Gaelic poets and they to me.' (*The Irish Times*) Born in County Limerick, Hartnett spent the later part of his life in Dublin. Linguistically, he remained rooted in Munster. Though not a native speaker himself, his grandmother was one of the last native Irish speakers of North Kerry and he felt linked through her to a betrayed Gaelic past. His poetic voice was born out of his research into that disappearing tradition. In 1975 he published *A Farewell to English*. *A Necklace of Wrens* (1987) presented poems from his Irish-language collections, together with their English translations in parallel text. 'I happen to think in two languages. I wake up at night thinking in two languages. It breaks my heart.' (*The Irish Times*) He translated the Hungarian poet Ferenc Juhász into Irish and Ó Bruadair, Haicéad, Ó Rathaille and Nuala Ní Dhomhnaill into English. For Peter Sirr, Hartnett 'had a psychological closeness to poets like Ó Bruadair, Ó Rathaille, who came from the broken Gaelic order and found themselves without an audience'. Two hundred and fifty years later, Hartnett gave them a new audience. Other works include *Anatomy of a Cliché* (1968) and *Inchicore Haiku* (1985).

DERMOT HEALY 1947–

'The hardest thing about writing the novel [*Sudden Times*, 1999] was sustaining the same tone throughout [the voice of a man returned from London's building sites to work in a Sligo supermarket] . . . I'd chosen to write in a voice that wouldn't let me stray from it. Descriptive passages, for example, were out. So it's written in a very different style to say, *Goat's Song*.' (to Rosita Boland, *The Irish Times*) As Healy has been described as writing 'in surprisingly different registers, even within the confines of a single story . . . sometimes lordly and ironic, at other times lyrical and precise' (*Field Day Anthology*), this must have been a particularly difficult straitjacket to confine himself within. Won two Hennessy Awards in the 1970s. First novel, *Fighting With Shadows*, was published in 1984. *A Goat's Song* – 'one of the best Irish novels of this decade' (John Kenny, *The Irish Times*) – won the 1994 Encore Award for best second novel. The autobiographical *The Bend For Home* appeared in 1996. Born in County Westmeath, now lives in Sligo. Has written for screen and stage. Has directed and acted in several plays and films. Other works include a poetry collection, *The Ballyconnell Colours* (1992).

JOHN HEALY 1930–1991

'We don't get mad anymore' – the phrase with which Healy began and ended his passionate account of the neglect by successive national administrations of his native Charlestown, County Mayo in *Death of an Irish Town* (first serialised in *The Irish Times* as *No One Shouted 'Stop'*). The book chronicled the devastating effect of emigration on the west. Those who were left were too numb to be mad. In 1967, Healy was made 'Mayoman of the Year' in recognition of his efforts to revive the west. Left school after the Intermediate Certificate to work as a reporter with the *Western People.* Moved to Dublin. Became (aged twenty-nine) editor of *The Sunday Review.* Subsequently worked on *The Irish Times* where he wrote the 'Backbencher' column for many years. Chaired 'The Hurler on the Ditch', a political panel discussion on television, and received a Jacob's Award for broadcasting (1967). In 1978 he published *Nineteen Acres*, an account of the struggle of his mother's family on a small Mayo holding, through a civil war, two world wars, economic depression and the economic 'rationalisation' of the seventies.

SEAMUS HEANEY 1939–

For Heaney, the form of a poem is 'crucial to poetry's power . . . to remind us that we are hunters and gatherers of values, that our very solitudes and distresses are creditable, in so far as they, too, are an earnest of our veritable human being.' ('Crediting Poetry', *Opened Ground*) In 1995, Heaney was awarded the Nobel Prize for Literature for his 'works of lyrical beauty and ethical depth'. The honour has not stifled him. Last year he won The Irish Times Poetry Section Literary Award for *Opened Ground*. This year, his translation of the Anglo-Saxon *Beowulf* brought him his second Whitbread Book of the Year Award, the last being for *The Spirit Level* in 1996. The eldest of nine children, Heaney grew up on a small farm in County Derry, 'an intimate, physical, creaturely existence', before going to Queen's University, Belfast. His first collections of poems *Death of a Naturalist*, *Door into the Dark*, *Wintering Out* reflected that deeply pastoral upbringing, an upbringing that has so suffused his being that it cannot but be the filter through which all his poetry passes. In an agenda-based critical climate, Heaney 'has been widely praised and harshly dismissed, and often misread.' (Eileen Battersby, *The Irish Times*)

AIDAN HIGGINS 1927–

'He has not done better than *Langrishe, Go Down*. Few have.' (Cóilín Owens, *Dictionary of Irish Writers*) The semi-lived existence of the Langrishe sisters, 1930s casualties of stagnation, had earlier been sketched in a short story, 'Killachter Meadow', from the prize-winning collection *Felo de Se* (later re-published as *Asylum and Other Stories*). In the novel (which won the James Tait Black Memorial Prize and an Irish Academy Award) the irrelevance of the women to anyone, even to themselves, is shown with meticulous and chilly care. It was subsequently adapted for BBC television by Harold Pinter. Higgins was born in County Kildare, but passed most of his childhood in County Dublin. He subsequently travelled extensively through Europe and Africa with a Marionette company. Has spent much of his adult life outside Ireland. Other works include *Balcony of Europe* (1972), which was a runner-up for the Booker Prize, *Scenes from a Receding Past* (1977), *Bornholm Night-ferry* (1983) and *Lions of the Grunewald* (1993). *Donkey's Years* (1995) and *Dog Days* (1997) are autobiographical and the latter 'plays hell with conventional time sequences in a virtuoso shuffling and reshuffling of past and present.' (Brian Fallon, *The Irish Times*)

RITA ANN HIGGINS 1955–

The poet and playwright is a native of Galway. In 1982 she joined a Galway writer's workshop and her first collection of poetry, *Goddess on the Mervue Bus*, was published in 1986. Received a writing bursary from the Arts Council in 1986 and a Peadar O'Donnell award in 1989. *Sunny Side Plucked* was a Poetry Society Recommendation. Her poems have been broadcast on RTÉ Radio, on BBC 4 and on television. She has read her poetry at home and abroad and it has been widely anthologised. Her play *Face Licker Come Home*, performed by the Punchbag Theatre Company at the Galway Arts Festival in 1991, was highly successful. Other plays include *God of the Hatch Man* and *Colie Lally Doesn't Live in a Bucket*. The poems, delivered briefly and with savage wit, expose hypocrisies of all sorts – political, social, sexual. She has been writer-in-residence in Galway Library, NUI, Galway and recently, as Offaly's writer-in-residence, Higgins edited an anthology of local writings, *Out of Clara Road* (1999), for Offaly County Council. She has held prison workshops in Portlaoise, Limerick, Cork and Loughan House. She has taught at Yale University. Other poetry collections include *Higher Purchase*, *Philomena's Revenge*, *Witch in the Bushes*.

On 30 September 1967, Judith and her family left their comfortable house for a 'new life in the mountains of Wales', where they lived without indoor plumbing and electricity (communication was by wind-powered radiophone). In 1981, they moved to County Donegal where she and her husband (a full-time landscape painter, who died last September at the end of a painting day) dedicated themselves to living a simple, sustainable lifestyle. *Need or Greed: Practical Choices* (1999), published by Gill and Macmillan (who also published *Healing with Herbs*), gives practical advice on how to achieve more appropriate ways of living, emphasising the power of the individual to effect change. Judith's first book, *This is Donegal Tweed* (1987) (which she published herself as Shoestring Publications – 'so named for obvious reasons!'), is considered the definitive work in the area. Judith spent many years working in textiles but at fifty-one she changed careers. Studied Chinese medicine in England, returning to Donegal with a diploma to practice. To that diploma, she 'glued on' her lay herbalism. In June 2000, she said goodbye to the first group to have completed her 'Living Earth Apprenticeship' and prepared to meet a new group.

'*The Leaves on Grey* [1980] contains the symbol which most appropriately sums up the nature of Hogan's art: the stained glass window, here the last act of creation by a dying artist, in which broken shards are fitted together and transformed by light into a vision of beauty, perfectly encapsulates the method – and the achievement – of this writer.' (Geoff Sadler, *Contemporary Novelists*) Hogan's first novel, *The Ikon Maker*, published originally by Co-op publications in 1976, was bleakly set in County Galway, where Hogan himself was born and grew up. His books describe loneliness and vulnerability in a language that can be startlingly original. In the 1970s he won a Hennessy Literary Award, The Rooney Prize and the Rhys memorial prize. During that decade he also graduated from University College, Dublin and acted with the Children's T Company theatre group. Other works include *A Curious Street* (1984), *A New Shirt* (1986) and, nine years later, *A Farewell to Prague* (1995). His four books of short stories are *The Diamonds at the Bottom of the Sea* (1979) *Children of Lir* (1981) *The Mourning Thief* and *Lebanon Lodge* (1988). *The Edge of the City* (1993) is a collection of journalistic pieces.

Born in Dublin, but moved to Spiddal some years ago. She writes in both Irish and English and a volume of her Irish poetry, *Dúrún*, was published in 1988, the year in which she won a Hennessy Award for the short story, 'Smile for Mammy'. Her play, *The Butterfly Who Couldn't Dance*, was performed at the Peacock in 1989 and she wrote TnaG's Ros na Rún soap opera in 1997. While director of the International Women Playwrights Conference, Galway in 1996, she and Ann Henning Jocelyn joined forces to form The Connemara Theatre Company. (This summer's project has been a work by the Norwegian, Jon Fosse (translated from Norwegian to English by Ann, and from English to Irish by Máire)). An unavoidable writing silence has been wonderfully ended since Holmes became first writer-in-residence on the Aran Islands for the year 2000. What has most surprised her is that she finds herself writing a novel in Irish. She is working on a film and has also written a choral piece, *Pax*, for forty voices at the request of Fergal Murray in conjunction with the Armagh Theatre Company. She is a shareholder (an honorary advisory position) of the Abbey Theatre.

A clinical pathologist and immunologist and also a leading poet, described by Ted Hughes as 'one of the half dozen most important poets writing anywhere'. Born in western Bohemia. After the Second World War (during which he worked on the railways) he studied science and medicine at Charles University, Prague. Started to write poetry as a student; and became editor of the scientific magazine, *Vesmír*. Published his first book of poems in 1954. Between 1970 and 1980 he became a non-person and his work was available only in translation. His poetry, controlled by an 'unromantic lyricism of the intellect' (Igor Hájek, *Contemporary World Writers*), is more deeply appreciated abroad than at home, where it has been regarded as 'finely accomplished applied art'. Works include *Notes of a Clay Pigeon* (1977), *Sindrom mizející plíce* ('Vanishing Lung Syndrome', 1990) and *Poems Before and After* (1990). Published more than 120 scientific papers and monographs. A book of his essays, *Shedding Life: Disease, Politics and other Human Conditions*, appeared in 1998. His works have been translated into thirty-seven languages. His scientific background is evident in his poetry which is both clinical and humane. Travelled widely. Visited the *Cúirt* festival in 1990.

'I fell in love with football as I was later to fall in love with women: suddenly, inexplicably, uncritically, giving no thought to the pain or disruption it would bring with it.' This may be the opening sentence of *Fever Pitch* (a compulsive read about an obsession) but it encapsulates the most pressing of Hornby's addictive concerns in all of his books – love, women, football and himself. Well – maybe it leaves out the music and a few more things besides. He succeeds in being both witty and poignant because he writes with a high degree of truth. *Fever Pitch*, a best-seller from its first publication in 1992, is not just an unassailable apologia for Arsenal fans, but an apologia for any football fan, or a genuine fan of anything whatsoever. *Fever Pitch* was made into a film, and Hornby has since published *High Fidelity* (1995) and *About a Boy* (1998) which were also widely praised. Worked as a teacher before turning to writing as a full-time career.

'Tá meas mór agam ar Raiftearaí. Fuair m'athair an céad duais san Oireachtas lena gearrscéalta sna blianta 1945 agus 1946. Scríobnoirí iontacha m'athair agus Raiftearaí. B'iad mo laochra móra.'

'Druid took Broadway by storm this week, picking up four Tony Awards. It's no overnight success – more the result of a 22-year commitment to excellence.' Mebh Ruane (*The Irish Times*) paying tribute to Druid and its director, Hynes, on their 1998 success with Martin McDonagh's play *The Beauty Queen of Leenane*. Born in County Roscommon – 'I didn't speak English until I went to school'. (to Eileen Battersby, *The Irish Times*) Founded the Druid Theatre in 1975 with fellow Galway graduates Mick Lally and Marie Mullen. First production, *The Playboy of the Western World*. In 1983 formed an association with Tom Murphy, producing *Conversations on a Homecoming* and *Bailegangaire*, both of which transferred to the West End. Her years as artistic director of the Abbey Theatre in the early 1990s were difficult for Hynes despite some outstanding successes. But her return to the Druid was explosive. 'If Martin McDonagh had not existed, Garry Hynes would have had to invent him . . . the trilogy is the culmination of a long demythologisation of the West that she and the company have conducted through such great productions as *The Playboy of the Western World*, M.J. Molloy's *The Wood of the Whispering* and Tom Murphy's *Bailegangaire* and *Conversations on a Homecoming*.' (Fintan O'Toole, *The Irish Times*)

Chairman of the Board of Trustees of the Ueno Gakuen Educational Foundation and President of Ueno Gakuen University in Tokyo. Began her career as a scholar of Anglo-Irish Literature, particularly of Yeats. Lectured twice at the Yeats Summer School in Sligo. Published one of the lectures, *W.B. Yeats and the Noh* (1966). She studied under T.R. Henn at Cambridge and visited and was guided by Mrs. W.B. Yeats. A member of the Chancellor's Court of Benefactors of Oxford University since 1990 and Honorary Fellow of St. Hilda's College, Oxford. While doubting that Yeats had possessed an overall idea of beauty sufficient to unify every element of the play (the words, music, costumes, settings, choreography) and pointing out that Yeats did not hesitate to introduce more than one type of beauty, as well as ugliness, Ishibashi concluded her study by saying that 'Yeats recognised the *Noh* as a form of poetic drama, and he created an entirely new form of his own . . . A creation . . . can be born of a misunderstanding. And a creative worker is free to turn misunderstanding into creation, if only his works have in themselves the power to exist as high art.'

P.D. JAMES 1920–

Creator of the detective and poet Adam Dalgliesh, the character central to her series of psychologically complex detective stories/novels. Her first book, *Cover Her Face*, was written when she was in her early forties, as part of her over-all efforts to support her family. She was brought up in Cambridge. Had to leave school at sixteen. Married during the Second World War. Her husband returned from war service mentally deranged by his experience, and spent most of the rest of his life in psychiatric care. She worked within the hospital administrative system until her husband's death in 1964, and subsequently became a civil servant in the criminal section of the Department of Home Affairs. By 1979 her writing career had become so successful that she was able to retire from the civil service. Many of her novels have been televised. Her works include *Shroud for a Nightingale* (1971), *An Unsuitable Job for a Woman* (1972), *Death of an Expert Witness* (1977), *Innocent Blood* (1980), *Devices and Desires* (1989), *Original Sin* (1994) and *A Certain Justice* (1997). She was made a life peer in 1991.

FRED JOHNSTON 1951–

Founder, in 1986, of *Cúirt*, Galway's annual poetry and literature festival. Received an Arts Council Bursary in Literature in 1988 and was appointed writer-in-residence to Galway Library. Reviews poetry and fiction for a large number of journals and newspapers and is a consultant editor for *First Editions*, the bi-monthly literary and arts magazine, edited by Romanian, Simion Dumitrache. Born in Belfast, he was educated there and in Toronto. Was a founder, with Neil Jordan and others, of the Irish Writers' Co-operative in the mid-1970s. Moved to Galway in 1977. Won a Hennessy Literary Award in 1972, and in 1981 and 1982 received *Sunday Independent* awards for poem and short story of the month. A novel, *Picture of a Girl in a Spanish Hat*, was published in 1979 but it is as a poet and reviewer that Johnston is better-known. Has published several collections of poetry, including *Life and Death in the Midlands*, *A Scarce Light*, *Song at the Edge of the World* and *Keeping the Night Watch*. His most recent collection, *True North*, was published by Salmon. '. . . certain of the poems affected me, like a good movie or a haunting piece of music can.' (Patrick Chapman)

JENNIFER JOHNSTON 1930–

Daughter of dramatist, Denis Johnston, and actress, Shelagh Richards, Johnston didn't publish her first book, *The Captains and the Kings*, until she was over forty. Has been described, on the strength of her first three novels, as a 'big house' writer, but the term is a simplification. In those novels, she used the 'big house' theme to explore, amongst other things, the loneliness and alienation created by circumstances outside the individual's control while the 'big house' of *The Invisible Worm* is a convenient shield for someone whose sense of dislocation and detachment has its roots in a personal childhood catastrophe. Trapped within their circumstances (historical or personal), Johnston's individuals attempt to carve some tiny sense of their own being. Christina Hunt Mahony (*Contemporary Irish Literature*) notes a progression 'from the male to female perspective, and to a greater concentration on the analysis of self instead of national, historical, familial, and even marital considerations.' Johnston spent her childhood in Dublin, but has lived in Derry for many years. Other novels include *The Gates*, *How Many Miles to Babylon?*, *The Old Jest* (Whitbread award), *Shadows on our Skin*, *The Illusionist* and *Two Moons*. She has also written several plays. *The Gingerbread Woman* is due this year.

NEIL JORDAN 1950–

Now widely known as a risk-taking, highly imaginative and successful film director (a difficult combination to achieve), Neil Jordan, born in Sligo, made his first artistic impact as a writer. His collection of short stories, *Night in Tunisia*, won a Guardian Fiction Prize. The novels, *The Past*, *The Dream of a Beast*, *Sunrise with Sea Monster*, showed him to be an exciting and innovative writer. Fortunately the quality of his films counteracts the deprivation suffered by his reading fans. They include *Angel*, *The Company of Wolves*, *Mona Lisa*, starring Bob Hoskins and Michael Caine, 'wonderfully slimy in support' (*Leonard Maltin's Movie & Video Guide*), the brilliantly disturbing *The Crying Game*, an Oscar winner, starring Stephen Rea and the haunting Jaye Davidson in a debut role (Jordan has said he thought about the storyline for *The Crying Game* for eight years before writing the script – *The Irish Times*), *Michael Collins* and Pat McCabe's *The Butcher Boy*. His recent widely acclaimed film, an adaptation of Graham Greene's *The End of the Affair* (with Ralph Fiennes as the novelist who falls in love with a married woman, Julianne Moore) disappointingly won only two Academy Award nominations. Won a Bafta Award for best-adapted screenplay.

JOHN B. KEANE 1928–

John B. Keane's work has always been deeply appreciated by the Irish public. The Abbey Theatre was slower to respond. Rejected his first play, *Sive* (1959). When it went on to win the All-Ireland Amateur Drama Festival, Ernest Blythe had to invite the Listowel drama group to stage it in the Abbey for a week. But it wasn't until the 1980s that the Abbey really took Keane on board. It would be 'a foolish national theatre that ignored the work of one of the most rooted and prolific of Irish playwrights.' (Joe Dowling, quoted in *The Irish Times*) Awarded a Gradam, The National Theatre Society's highest award (1998) for his 'considerable contribution' to Irish Theatre. Born Listowel, County Kerry, he has, apart from a brief spell in England, lived there all his life. Major plays include *Many Young Men of Twenty*, *Moll*, *Big Maggie*, and, most memorably, *The Field*, a powerful play, made into an equally powerful film. He is also a novelist, a short-story writer and a poet. During his seventieth birthday party celebrations in his own pub in Listowel, RTÉ producer, Séamus Hosey, praised Keane's ability to turn 'the parochial and the particular into the universal work of art'.

SEÁN KEATING 1889–1977

In 1968, Des Kenny went to Keating and told him he was going to open the first art gallery in the West, and would like to start with a Keating show. 'I'm too old,' said Keating, 'not very mobile, tired, and I am artistically dead – nobody is interested in my work anymore'. The Salthill Gallery opened in July 1968 with Seán's exhibition, and hosted two more before he died. One of the openings coincided with an electricity strike – the gallery was festooned with tilly lamps, the customers carried candles and catalogues, there was a different kind of electricity in the air, and fifty-five Keating drawings were sold. From Limerick, Keating studied under Orpen. In 1915 his 'Men of the West' was shown at the RHA exhibition. Keating and others were 'hailed with some excitement as the first genuinely Irish school of painting, a new art reflecting both the realities and the aspirations of the new state and its citizens.' (Brian Fallon, *An Age of Innocence*) He was introduced to the Aran Islands by his friend and fellow artist, Harry Clarke. The place and the people were to provide the subject matter for some of his most deeply felt art.

BRIAN KEENAN 1950–

'During my captivity I, like my fellow hostages, was forced to confront the man I thought I was and to discover that I was many people. I had to befriend these many people, discover their origins, introduce them to each other and find a communality between themselves and myself.' (Brian Keenan, *An Evil Cradling*) As a Beirut hostage, Belfast-born Keenan spent four and a half years in captivity. His book describes the conditions in which he and his fellow hostages had to survive. The mental strength of Keenan and Englishman, John McCarthy, with whom he bonded so closely, shines throughout it. Keenan, who left school at the age of fifteen, graduated from the New University of Ulster. He taught in Belfast and in Europe before going to Beirut in 1986. *An Evil Cradling* won the *Irish Times* prize for non-fiction, the Christopher Ewart-Biggs memorial prize and the *Time/Life* international prize. In 1992, McCarthy, Keenan and Terry Waite were awarded the CBE. Frank McGuiness's play, *Someone Who'll Watch Over Me*, set in a prison cell, is dedicated to Brian Keenan. *Between Extremes* (1999) is the gentle account of a two-month holiday with McCarthy in Chile and a friendship which survived into the 'normality' of freedom.

JIM KEMMY 1936–1997

'His life was a crusade for the poor and disadvantaged. When elected mayor of Limerick he donated his salary of £16,000 to help local organisations.' (Boylan, *Dictionary of Irish Biography*) Stonemason, trade unionist, socialist, writer, Kemmy was born in Limerick. After completing his apprenticeship in the family stonemason business, he went to London. On his return in 1960, he worked as a stone mason for Limerick Corporation and began his lifetime commitment to politics, joining the Labour Party in 1963. In 1972 he left to form his own independent socialist group. An advocate of the separation of church and state and chairman of the Limerick Family Planning Clinic, he came into conflict with the church over the issues of contraception and abortion. Edited the *Limerick Socialist* 1972–1981. Became an independent TD for the first time in 1981. Founded the Democratic Socialist Party in 1982. In the early 1990s he led his Party into a merger with Labour. Was chairman of the Labour Party for the last five years of his life. A lover of literature and history, he edited the *Old Limerick Journal* and two anthologies, *The Limerick Anthology* and its companion, *The Limerick Compendium*.

'Your Excellency's Petitioner is the wife of Hugh Larkin who was sent out to New South Wales under the Rule of Transportation for life, from Galway Assizes . . . Petitioner begs of your Excellency to look with the eyes of pity on herself and children and order them a free passage to New South Wales'. This document concerning the man from whom his wife is descended stimulated Keneally to write *The Great Shame: A Story of the Irish in the Old World and the New* (1998). 'He has transmuted the raw material of diaries, letters, newspapers and recollections into a brilliant tapestry in which all the colours of its century [the nineteenth] glow as if they had been spun only yesterday.' (John Horgan, *The Irish Times*) Keneally is probably best-known for his tour-de-force, *Schindler's Ark* (Booker Prize in 1982, subsequently basis of film, *Schindler's List*). Used the 'texture and devices' of a novel to tell the story of flamboyant businessman Oskar Schindler's rescue of Jews from the Holocaust 'because the novel's techniques seem suited for a character of such ambiguity and magnitude as Oskar'. Born in Sydney, Keneally entered a seminary at seventeen, but left before ordination. He has written more than twenty novels.

His fourth Albany-based novel, *Ironweed*, about an alcoholic vagrant, won the Pulitzer prize and the National Book Critics Circle Award. It was subsequently made into an overly-long, but memorably-acted film starring Jack Nicholson and Meryl Streep. Since then, he has written *Quinn's Book* (a Dickensian descent into that period of American history from 1849–1864), *Very Old Bones* (1992), and *The Flaming Corsage* (1996). In 1984 he co-wrote a screenplay, *The Cotton Club*, with Francis Ford Coppola. He co-authored two children's books with his son Brendan Kennedy, *Charlie Malarkey and the Belly Button Machine* (1986) and *Charlie Malarkey and the Singing Moose* (1994). From Albany, New York, Kennedy graduated from Siena College, Loudonville, New York. He worked as a journalist in San Juan, Puerto Rico. Moved back to Albany in 1963 to concentrate on his writing (though not to the exclusion of journalism). Was Professor of English and Director of the New York State Writers' Institute at the State University of New York at Albany.

'As I write, I know that I am involved in an activity which is a deliberate assertion of energy over indifference, of vitality over deadness, of excitement and ecstasy over dullness and cynicism.' (Kennelly, quoted in *Contemporary Poets*) It is difficult to imagine Kennelly ever having to combat dullness. As well as being an exceptionally talented poet, a playwright and a novelist, Kennelly is Professor of Modern Literature in Trinity College, Dublin, where he began lecturing in the early 1960s. From Kerry, Kennelly came to Dublin in the 1950s. He interrupted his studies to work in the ESB and London, but returned before too long to academic life. He has lectured extensively in the US, and is possibly the only poet to have advertised cars (for Toyota) on TV. Was awarded AE Memorial Prize for Poetry 1967 and Critic's Special Harvey Award 1988. Much of his early work, both poetry and novels, was published by the Dublin publishing house, Allen Figgis. His poetry publications include *Moloney Up and At It, Cromwell, The Book of Judas, Love of Ireland – Poems from the Irish*. Plays include adaptations of *Antigone* and *Medea*.

At eighty, Kiely, in conversation with Eileen Battersby (*The Irish Times*), confessed to having three unfinished novels. 'It can be hard to finish a novel. I keep tinkering with them and I hope to have at least one of them finished. What can you do?' From Omagh, County Tyrone, Kiely, after a brief interlude as a Jesuit novitiate and an eighteen-month period in hospital, went to University College, Dublin. Since then he has worked as a writer. Was literary editor for *The Irish Press* in 1950. During the 1960s he spent five years in the US where he taught creative writing and wrote for several periodicals. His fiction spans several decades. His first novel, *Land without Stars*, was published in 1946. Three of his early novels were banned. In the 1950s, 'if you weren't banned, you were no bloody good'. His writing has taken careful note of change in Ireland. With *Proxopera* and *Nothing Happens in Carmincross* he confronted the invasion of violence into ordinary lives. '[S]ufficiently focused and extensive critical examinations of Kiely's recent, political fiction are lacking.' (Andrew Haggerty, *Modern Irish Writers*) Last summer, he published *The Waves Behind Us – Further Memories*, sequel to *Drink to the Bird*.

'I think all writing looks for truth . . . I hate making claims for profundity . . . I would say my plays are concerned with cutting through illusion. But I'm also aware that it's a kind of fruitless exercise. As we're constantly surrounded by illusion everywhere, in theatre and life.' (Kilroy to Eileen Battersby, *Irish Times*) Although his novel, *The Big Chapel* (1971), was short-listed for the Booker Prize, Kilroy's work since that time has been mainly as a dramatist. *The Death and Resurrection of Mr. Roche* (1969) views, through Roche's homosexuality, contrasting levels of self-awareness and acceptance amongst the different characters. Resigned the chair of English at NUI, Galway in 1989, to concentrate on writing. Other plays include *Talbot's Box, Double Cross, The Secret Fall of Constance Wilde*. Did acclaimed adaptations of Chekov's *The Seagull* and Ibsen's *Ghosts*. Director of Field Day Theatre Company from 1988–92. Resigned because 'I wanted it to be even more political. I felt that in a way what was needed of Field Day was the necessity to imagine an Ireland that has never existed and I still feel that is still the need of the moment.' (Kilroy to Battersby, 1997)

It must have been from Grandmother Mackenzie that King acquired his indefatigable zest for life. She, at seventy-five, learned to ski. In 'the older part of her old age' she took to sailing a yawl round the coast of Scotland. Preparatory school and Dartmouth Royal Naval College inured him against privation, luckily, as he underwent the unique experience of spending the entire war as operational commander of a submarine. His book, *The Stick and the Stars* (reissued as *Dive and Attack*), describes the strain of being part of a group of men submerged in a confined space, in constant danger. After the war he retired from the Navy and came to County Galway, where he farmed and hunted with the Galway Blazers. Eventually King was drawn back to sea. In the *Galway Blazer 11*, he sailed solo around the world, though not without mishap. On his first attempt, he hit a hurricane in the South Atlantic, the boat rolled over and was dismasted. On the next attempt he was rammed by a great white shark off the Australian coast, but managed to keep going after repairs. Recently he has slowed down and merely does a little mountaineering and skiing. (And in 1997 he published a novel, *Kamikaze: The Wind of God*.)

His contemporary, John Montague, describes the later Kinsella (as evidenced in *One* and *Fifteen Dead*) as 'one of the darkest, strongest, least accommodating poets around, with a rare integrity.' (*Contemporary Poets*) His father worked as a cooper for Guinness's Brewery in Dublin and Kinsella grew up in the city surrounded by an extensive family network. Worked in the Civil Service for nearly twenty years, publishing *Another September* and *Downstream* during that time. In 1965 he visited Southern Illinois University as writer-in-residence. *Wormwood* and *Nightwalker* were published in 1966 and 1967. After he became Professor of English in Temple University, Philadelphia in 1970, his work became more introspective and less lyrical. A director in the Dolmen and Cuala Presses, he was the founder of Peppercanister (which has published all his poetry since *Butcher's Dozen*). *Blood and Family* (1988) collected together all the Peppercanister poems of the previous decade. In 1972 '*Notes from the Land of the Dead* appeared in a limited edition, and from that moment an indeflectible exploration of the self and its agons was under way in this poet's work.' (Seamus Heaney, *Watching the River Flow: A Century in Irish Poetry*)

The reclusive poet and artist, Pascal L'Estrange, first came to public attention several years ago. Prised with difficulty from his Connemara retreat of twenty years, he was persuaded to launch his work, *The Affirmative Negative*, in the intimacy of Kennys' Bookshop. Dressed, most unreclusively, in a Stetson hat, cravat, and long 'flasher's' overcoat, he stunned guests with a long selection of poems on such diverse topics as nuns' thighs and rocket fuel. The work was thought by some to be no more than gibberish, but others, more attuned to the experimental in verse, appreciated the raw energy emanating from the poet's entire artistic persona. Such was the interest in this new figure, both locally and nationally, that RTÉ television invited a panel of well-known personalities to comment on an exhibition of L'Estrange's paintings, which, unlike his flamboyant verse, were austere canvases of black on white. They were entranced and spoke with abstruse seriousness on the nature of this newfound art (the artist/poet himself was occasionally to be seen flitting nervously and speechlessly across the room). The next day, Tom Kenny could have sold 700 copies of *The Affirmative Negative* had he had them to hand. Unfortunately the book, like Pascal L'Estrange, had been conceived on April 1st and no copies were available.

MARY LAVIN 1912–1996

'The imagination cannot be trusted unless it is fully disciplined. When it is so disciplined, its blinding light shuts out all that is irrelevant.' (Mary Lavin, *Tales from Bective Bridge*, 1996). The short story writer was born in Massachusetts to Irish parents. Came to Ireland at the age of ten. Graduated from University College, Dublin. Gave up work on a PhD to concentrate on writing (received an honorary doctorate from UCD in 1968). Her first collection, *Tales from Bective Bridge*, won the James Tait Black Memorial Prize in 1943. 'The stories are subversive, dangerous even, in the way that human relationships, devoid of sincerity or morality, can themselves be. These complex pictures are not tales or anecdotes, they are instead fully-fledged, shocking reminders of how life is and has always been.' (Evelyn Conlon, introducing 1996 republication of *Tales from Bective Bridge*) Throughout her career, Lavin published nineteen collections of short stories and was a regular contributor to the *New Yorker*. Linking Lavin's work to the American spirit of independence, Professor Maurice Harmon commented that Lavin widows are 'capable, life-affirming women' who 'refuse to become passive and pitiful. They have the courage to roll the stone away from the tomb.'

EDDIE LENIHAN 1950–

'You watch Irish dancers, you listen to Irish music, but when did you last listen to a good Irish story?' The ancient tradition of storytelling is being lost in this country, but Lenihan, who specialises in 'horrible, vicious, brutal tales' on diverse themes (ferocious Irish women, the Devil – you can find a theme on anything in Irish folklore, even porridge), is fighting a brilliant rear-guard action. A celebrated storyteller, Lenihan has not only written fifteen books for adults and children, but has recorded many tapes and CDs here and in the US, including (for Claddagh Records) *The Devil's Own Work* and the recent double CD, *Storyteller*. A series of Ten Minute Tales for RTÉ was subsequently brought out on video. Lenihan, a teacher, has spent the last twenty-six years collecting folklore. From Kerry, he now lives in County Clare. Introducing *Gruesome Irish Tales for Children* (telling of the all-too-human hero, Fionn MacCumhail) Lenihan says that 'terror is never more than a few steps away, lurking in the shadows. But there is humour too, and kindness, and the comradeship that is necessary if such obstacles are to be overcome. And if they are conquered it is never without a price being paid or some lesson learned.'

HUGH LEONARD 1926–

The memoir, *Home Before Night*, describes Leonard's (a.k.a. John Byrne) childhood and youth in the County Dublin village of Dalkey (where he still lives). An extremely popular and prolific playwright, his first international success was with *Stephen D*, an adaptation of Joyce's *A Portrait of the Artist as a Young Man* and *Stephen Hero* (produced Dublin (1962), London (1963), New York (1967)), but probably his greatest triumph was with *Da*, (drawing, like *Home Before Night*, from Leonard's own life) which won several Tony awards when it was produced on Broadway, and was subsequently made into a film (1987). Other plays include *Time Was, A Life* (in which a minor character from *Da* comes centre stage), *Kill, The Mask of Moriarty* (famed for the fact that the plot of the play was revealed in advance of its opening at the 1985 Dublin Theatre Festival) and *Love in the Title*. Leonard has worked extensively in theatre and television, adapting works such as *The Irish RM* (Somerville and Ross), *Strumpet City* (James Plunkett), Jennifer Johnston's *The Captains and the Kings* (as *The Last Campaign*) and *Good Behaviour* (Molly Keane). Was a columnist for *The Sunday Independent*. Reviews for *The Irish Times*.

ANITA LESLIE 1914–1985

'In my parents' view schools performed the same function that kennels did for dogs. They were places where pets could be conveniently deposited while their owners travelled.' (*The Gilt and the Gingerbread*) Schooling was intermittent for the future biographer, who was still unable to read at the age of eight. Her mother was an 'American belle, bred of pioneer stock' and her father, Shane Leslie, was an 'Anglo-Irish man of letters from County Monaghan'. (Her great grandmother was a Red Indian – Bill King.) During the Second World War, she joined the French Army as an ambulance driver because it was the only army to allow women to drive in the front line. (*A Story Half Told*) In 1945, the 1st French Armoured Division crossed the Rhine, and Leslie drove one of the twelve ambulances which accompanied the tanks, armoured cars and infantry. She met her future husband, submarine commander, Bill King, in the Lebanon during the war and afterwards they came to Ireland. For many years they lived in Oranmore Castle, County Galway. Amongst her other works are *Jennie: The Life of Lady Randolph Churchill* (Leslie's great-aunt), *Cousin Clare* (her father's cousin, Clare Sheridan) and *Edwardians in Love*.

DENISE LEVERTOV 1923–1997

Although born and raised in Ilford, Essex, Levertov was regarded as a quintessentially American poet. Her mother was Welsh and her father a Russian Jew who settled in England after the First World War and became an Anglican priest. Levertov was educated at home. Worked as a nurse in London during Second World War. First collection, *The Double Image*, was published in London, 1946. Emigrated to the US in 1948. *With Eyes at the Back of Her Head* (1959) established her reputation in America. A political activist as well as a poet, she campaigned on many social issues. 'It was important to her to go and protest . . . It's like she was very nineteenth century with her vision of what poetry was and how total a calling it was.' (Barbara Epler, Levertov's editor, *Houston Chronicle*) One of the most highly regarded women poets, her poetry is deeply infused with spirituality. While writing about desires, needs and wants, 'the myth she is working out in all the poems is that of the Garden' (Diane Wakoski, *Contemporary Poets*) where desires, needs and wants disappear. Her works include *Collected Earlier Poems 1940–1960, Poems 1960–1967, Selected Poems* (1986), *Breathing the Water, A Door in the Hive*.

PATRICK LINDSAY 1914–1993

Barrister and politician and noted wit, Lindsay published the autobiographical *Memories* shortly before his death. He was born in Dublin, but his parents moved back to a small farm in their local Mayo before he reached school age. He graduated from University College, Galway. He was called to the Bar in 1946. Became senior counsel and was elected Fine Gael TD for North Mayo in 1954. 'Pat had that rare ability to be as partisan and rabid a Fine Gaeler as one could find – an unrepentant Blueshirt – while making and keeping friends on all sides.' (Drapier, *The Irish Times*) Parliamentary secretary for the Departments of Education and the Gaeltacht, becoming Minister for the Gaeltacht in 1956. Government lost power in 1957. Lindsay was re-elected. After his defeat in the 1961 election, he became Leas-Cathaoirleach in the Senate (1961–65). Failed to take a seat in Dublin North-Central in 1969. Resumed his legal career. 'As a negotiator in the Round Hall of the Four Courts, he performed like an amiable bear gobbling up Insurance claims' men as if they were smarties.' (*Dli*) From 1975–1984 he held the position of Master of the High Court.

MORGAN LLYWELYN 1937–

A writer of extremely well-researched and vivid main-line historical fiction, based on Irish legends and historical events. Llywelyn was born in New York. She began to write in the 1970s, and her first book, *The Wind From Hastings*, was published in 1978. Through her research, she became increasingly interested in Celtic life. In 1981, she had her name legally changed to Llywelyn. On the death of her husband in 1985, she moved permanently to Ireland. She has written award-winning fiction for both adults and children. *The Horse Goddess* was named best novel of 1983 by the National League of American Pen Women and Best Novel for Young Adults by the American Library Association. *Brian Boru* (1990) and *Strongbow* (1992) both won Bisto Awards for Excellence in Children's Literature. Other works include *Lion of Ireland* (1980) and its sequel, *Pride of Lions* (1996), *Grania* (1986), *On Raven's Wing* (1990). Some of her books, such as *The Elementals* (1993), are sheer fantasy. She has written books in collaboration with Michael Scott.

LIZ LOCHHEAD 1947–

Poet and playwright. Born in Motherwell. Studied at the Glasgow School of Art. She taught art for eight years before turning to writing full-time. Talking some years ago about her interest in 'people's darker natures', she told her interviewer 'I'm very interested in repression of various sorts, linguistic, sexual, whatever. I keep thinking of a line from a poem by Adrienne Rich: "*A thinking woman sleeps with monsters . . .*"' (talking to Rebecca Wilson, *Sleeping With Monsters*) She is editorial director of *Polygon*. Works include *Blood and Ice* (1982), *Dracula* (1985), *Memo for Spring* (1972), *Dreaming Frankenstein and Collected Poems*, (1984), *True Confessions and New Clichés, Mary Queen of Scots Got Her Head Chopped Off*. Her play, *Perfect Days*, a 'sharp and poignant comedy' about a thirty-nine year old Glaswegian celebrity hairdresser who wants, above all, to have a baby (performed by the Traverse Theatre Company), recently played at the Vaudeville Theatre in London's West End and was nominated for a Laurence Olivier Theatre Award 2000. *Cuba/Dog House* is to be published later this year.

Longley has referred to '. . . the problematic condition of Irish criticism itself – indexed to the political arguments of the last seventy-five years . . . ' .One of Ireland's most noted critics, Edna Longley is married to the poet, Michael Longley. She was born in Cork, educated in Trinity College, Dublin and is currently Professor of English at Queen's University, Belfast. Edited Edward Thomas' *Poems and Last Poems* (1973). She has also edited *The Selected James Simmons* (1978) and *The Selected Paul Durcan* (1982 and 1985). In *Poetry in the Wars* (1986) Longley argues that '[p]oetry and politics, like church and state, should be separated. And for the same reasons: mysteries distort the rational processes which ideally prevail in social relations; while ideologies confiscate the poet's special passport to *terra incognita*.' In 1988, she wrote a book on the poet Louis MacNeice who, in her view, 'did more than other twentieth-century poets to test poetry against the century.' Other works include *The Living Stream: Literature and Revisionism in Ireland* (1994), *Across a Roaring Hill: the Protestant Imagination in Modern Ireland* (co-edited with Gerald Dawe, 1985), *From Cathleen to Anorexia: The Breakdown of Ireland* (1990).

'Though the poet's first duty must be to his imagination, he has other obligations – and not just as a citizen. He would be inhuman if he did not respond to tragic events in his own community, and a poor artist if he did not seek to endorse that response imaginatively . . . In the context of political violence the deployment of words at their most precise and suggestive remains one of the few antidotes to death-dealing dishonesty.' (to Eileen Battersby, *The Irish Times*) Born Belfast, of English parents, Longley studied classics under W.B. Stanford in Trinity College, Dublin. Worked in the Arts Council of Northern Ireland until 1991, the year he won the Whitbread Poetry Prize for *Gorse Fires* (his first collection in twelve years). His new collection, *The Weather in Japan*, for which he was awarded the Hawthornden Prize, was published this year. A poet of formality, lyrical intensity and wide-ranging links. Much of his poetry is concerned with the intrusion of violence into personal lives. 'Ceasefire', written in the early 1990s, spells out the depth of the sacrifice which reconciliation demands. 'I get down on my knees and do what must be done/And kiss Achilles' hand, the killer of my son.'

'Thomas Lynch looks into the eyes of corpses and sees their lives and their difficult loves that remind him of his own. And he manages to do this with humour and grace . . .' . (Matthew Sweeney of the collection *Grimalkin and Other Poems*, 1994) Lynch knows more about death than most poets. He is an undertaker from Milford, Michigan. He divides his time between Michigan (where he is Rotarian and former President of the Chamber of Commerce) and his great greatgrandfather's house in Moveen, County Clare. He has been coming to Ireland for thirty years. As well as poetry, he has published a volume of essays (which won the American Book Award) *The Undertaking – Life Studies from the Dismal Trade*. 'The book is so good you could be reading Montaigne.' (John Boland, *The Irish Times*) 'With the essays, I'm trying to do something different. There is a polemical intent. I think the essays are trying to say we learn lessons about our living from the facts of our mortality. I guess I'm trying to help people look at something we don't like confronting. About four or five people will die in this county alone tonight.' (Lynch to Eileen Battersby, *The Irish Times*)

Although born in Galway, Mac Amlaigh's childhood was spent in Kilkenny after the transfer of his father, an army sergeant, to that city. He left school before he was sixteen. Following a brief spell in the army himself, he emigrated to England to work as a labourer in 1951. He remained there for the rest of his life. Prionsias Mac Aonghusa is currently editing an Irish-language diary, 'extending to over a million words' (Boylan, *Dictionary of Irish Biography*), which Mac Amlaigh maintained on a daily basis for more than thirty years. His works include *Dialann Deoraí* (1960), which was published in translation as *An Irish Navvy* in 1964, *Saol Saighdiúra* (1962), *Diarmaid Ó Dónaill* (1965), which was a Club Leabhar selection, *Sweeney agus Scéalta Eile* (1970), *Schnitzer Ó Sé* (1974) and *Beoir Bhaile* (1981). Mac Amlaigh wrote both in English and Irish for *The Irish Times* and other newspapers. RTÉ showed his award-winning television drama *Saighdiúirí* in 1965, but 'he remains essentially the most important literary witness to the pain and endurance of mid-century Irish emigrants forced by economic circumstances to find work in post-war Britain.' (*Modern Irish Lives*)

'It is said that too perfect an upbringing unfits one for adult life. It may be true, but I would not barter my golden childhood and adolescence for any possible alternative – well, the mythical exchange of *Éire, Gaelach agus gan roinn* ('Ireland, Gaelic and undivided') might tempt me, but failing that, nothing.' (Máire Mhac an tSaoi, *Southern Review*) An Irish language poet, her first collection, *Margadh na Saoire*, was published in 1956 to great acclaim. Born in Dublin. Spent much of her childhood in her uncle's retreat in the Kerry Gaeltacht. Educated at University College, Dublin and the Sorbonne. A scholar at the Dublin Institute for Advanced Studies. Qualified as a barrister, joined the diplomatic service and travelled abroad extensively. Married Conor Cruise O'Brien. Recently published *Shoa agus Dánta Eile*. Talking to poet Mary O'Malley (*The Irish Times*), the scholar and poet confessed, surprisingly, that she hadn't taken her writing sufficiently seriously. 'I owed it to those who saw to it that I knew the language well, I owed it to them to put it to better use. I feel that strongly as an older woman.' Other works include *Codladh an Ghaiscígh, An Galar Dubhach, An Cíom Go Dtí Seo*.

A native Irish speaker from Casla, Connemara. He has spent all his working life in Dublin. Taught both in Scoil Lorcáin (an all-Irish primary school in Monkstown) and in the Irish Language Laboratory in University College, Dublin. Spent eleven years as a journalist and nearly thirty years as newsreader with RTÉ. Has chaired and presented the language programme, 'Leagan Cainte' since its inception in 1995. His deep commitment to the Irish language has led to such publications as *Conamara, An Tir Aineoil* with photographer Bob Quinn (1997), while he has translated two of the map-maker and geographer Tim Robinson's books, *Mapping South Connemara* (*Conamara Theas – Áit agus Ainm*, 1992) and *Space, Time and Connemara* (*Spás, Am, Conamara*, 1993). His translation of some seventeenth to nineteenth century Irish poetry was published in *Taisce Duan* (1992). He contributed biographical sketches of traditional singers in Irish to *A Companion to Irish Traditional Music*, edited by Fintan Valelly (1999), produced *Ireland Of The Proverbs* with photographer Bill Doyle (1988) and has recently published a biography of Breandán Ó hEithir, *Ionramh Aonair – Breandán Ó hEithir, Beatháisnéis* (2000).

In the year 2000 Mac Aonghusa received a Lifetime Achievement in Journalism Award at the Oireachtas. He has, over the years, been columnist for a variety of publications, including *The Irish Times, The Sunday Press, The Sunday Independent, Feasta, Comhar* and *Foinse*. He was Ireland Correspondent for *New Statesman* for a decade. His fifteen books include studies of The Gaelic League (*Ar Son na Gaeilge*), proportional representation (*PR in Ireland*), Éamon de Valera (*Éamon de Valera, Na Blianta Réabhlóideacha*) and the IRA in Connemara (*Ros Muc agus Cogadh na Saoirse*). He has been presenter, editor and producer on radio and television at intervals since 1952 and his career has allowed him to travel widely. In 1974/75 he represented the United Nations in South Central Africa. His immediate superior was Seán McBride, with whom he collaborated on many enterprises over the years. He spent his early years in the Connemara Gaeltacht. His mother was imprisoned in Galway Jail and later in Kilmainham Jail in 1922/23 for her Republican activities. His main interest is in the restoration of the Irish Language. Founder of Amharclann de hÍde, the first professional Irish language theatre. He is married to Supreme Court Justice, Catherine McGuinness.

Described by Peter Porter (*Contemporary Poets*) as 'the most inventive poet of his generation in Britain.' Born in Lanarkshire, graduated from Oxford. His first book of poems, *A Form of Words*, came out in 1954. Many publications followed. Won the Faber Memorial Award, 1964. Edited *Poet's Voice* (1958-65), *New Comment* (1959-64) and *Poetry Now* (1965-76). Soon after the appearance of his *Collected Poems* in 1971, he left BBC radio. His first novel, *The Transformation*, was published in 1975. He wrote a number of novels amongst which a series of 'openly erotic fantasies' (Porter) brought him 'public success' as a prose writer. Received the Cholmondeley Award, 1977. MacBeth moved to County Galway in the late 1980s and his response to the place can be glimpsed in his collection of poems, *Trespassing: Poems from Ireland*, which MacBeth intended to contain, as well as an admiration for 'the sinuosities of the tongue', 'an undercurrent of willingness to wrestle with the complex and bitter legacy of the planters, the English and Scottish land-owners who have trespassed in Ireland down the years.' (MacBeth) Other works include *Poems of Love and Death, Anatomy of a Divorce* and *Collected Poems 1958–1982*.

WALTER MACKEN 1915–1967

Macken's achievements point to a life much longer than the fifty-one years he actually lived. Not only a novelist and a dramatist, Macken was also an accomplished actor on stage (both with the Taibhdhearc and the Abbey) and in film (he played a leading role in Brendan Behan's *The Quare Fellow*). For nine years he was actor/manager/director of the Gaelic Theatre (which subsequently became Galway's famous Taibhdhearc), producing translations of Shakespeare, O'Casey, Capek, Shaw and Ibsen. During the 1940s and 1950s he wrote several plays, acting the leading role in the best known of them, *Home is The Hero*, on Broadway in 1954. His 'greater growth as a dramatist was limited mainly by his considerable success as a novelist and his increasing fascination with fiction.' (*Dictionary of Irish Literature*) He was briefly artistic director and manager of the Abbey Theatre in 1966. His first two novels, *I Am Alone* and *Rain on the Wind*, were banned during the time of most oppressive censorship in Ireland. 'At his best, as in his study of Claddagh fishermen, *Rain on the Wind*, Macken is not only powerful but memorable.' (*Dictionary of Irish Literature*) He later wrote the wide-ranging historical trilogy, *Seek The Fair Land*, *The Silent People* and *The Scorching Wind*.

BERNARD MACLAVERTY 1942–

His two best-known works are *Lamb* (his first novel, published in 1980) and *Cal* (1983), both of which were subsequently made into films, the former starring Liam Neeson and Hugh O'Connor, the latter with Helen Mirren, Donal McCann and Ray McAnally. He writes about tenderness, passion and guilt with great empathy and subtlety and without any reliance on special effects. A quiet, totally engrossing writer. MacLaverty was born in Belfast. He spent ten years as a laboratory technician at Queen's University, Belfast before taking a degree in English. Moved to Scotland to teach. His first book, *Secrets and Other Stories* (1977), won a Scottish Arts Council Award. *Lamb* was short-listed for a *Guardian* Fiction Prize. His short story, 'My Dear Palestrina', was adapted both for BBC television and radio. MacLaverty lived on the Isle of Islay, off the west coast of Scotland, for some time, as did the troubled female composer in his 1997 novel, *Grace Notes* (the first since *Cal* and short-listed for the Booker Prize). Other works include *A Time to Dance*, *The Great Profundo* and *Walking the Dog*.

SORLEY MACLEAN (SOMHAIRLE MACGILL-EAIN) 1911–1996

'During the 1930s I was obsessed with politics . . . what poetry I wrote was full of conflict. Much of it was a quarrel with myself for my lack of single-mindedness.' (MacLean) Iain Crichton Smith, translator of MacLean's *Dain do Eimhir* (*Poems to Eimhir*), regarded him as the most original Gaelic poet of the twentieth century. He saw a poet opening up Gaelic poetry to a world 'beyond purely parochial boundaries'. Born on the island of Raasay, Gaelic was MacLean's first language. Went to school on Skye. Studied English at Edinburgh University. Served in North Africa during the Second World War and was wounded three times. After the war, he returned to teaching, becoming headmaster of Plockton Secondary School, Wester Ross, in 1956, a position he held until his retirement. Was instrumental in preserving Gaelic in Scottish schools during the 1960s. Founder of the School for Scottish Studies in Edinburgh. Received the Queen's Gold Medal for poetry in 1990. *O Choille gu Bearradh/From Wood to Ridge: Selected Poems in Gaelic and English*, was published in parallel text with MacLean's own translations in 1989. '[A]n important venture in itself as well as a courageous one.' (Brian Fallon, *The Irish Times*)

BRYAN MACMAHON 1909–1998

'Bryan was in love with people. Encounters, speech, conversation, were the lifeblood that sustained, nurtured and gave him such pleasure.' (His son, Maurice, to *The Irish Times*) This zest for humanity was reflected in his widespread and deeply rooted interests. As well as being a novelist, short story writer, dramatist and folklorist, MacMahon was also a collector of music and song, a raconteur and an authority on Shelta, the language of the travelling community. A schoolteacher for more than forty years, he lived and worked throughout his life in North Kerry. He was instrumental in the birth of the Listowel Writers' Week. Works include *The Honey Spike* (first performed in the Abbey Theatre, 1961, and based on two young travellers expecting their first child), the novel, *Children of the Rainbow* (1952), an oral memoir, *The Master* (1992), and *A Final Fling*, a short story collection, published just before his death. 'Ever the teacher, he wanted his fiction to entertain, teach and, above all, explain the complexities and contradictions of Ireland, her attitudes and her people, to the Irish and to others.' (Eileen Battersby, *The Irish Times*) Maurice recorded his father's voice on tape over a fifteen-year period. The collection forms a unique archive.

DEIRDRE MADDEN 1960–

Madden won a Hennessy Literary Award in 1980, when she was still a student at Trinity College, Dublin. In 1987 she was awarded the Rooney Prize for Irish Literature. Her first novel, *Hidden Symptoms*, was published in Faber's *First Fictions* anthology, *Introduction 9*. *Birds of the Innocent Wood*, published in the same year, won the Somerset Maugham Prize. She has been widely praised for her fine and poetic prose style. Her central characters tend to be women, and she writes of their internal stresses and struggles to create meaning from their lives with great perception. From Toome Bridge, County Antrim, she was educated at Trinity and the University of East Anglia. She currently lives in France. During the 1990s she has written three further novels, *Remembering Light and Stone* (1992), *Nothing Is Black* (1994) and *One by One in the Dark*, her fifth novel, which is set on the eve of the IRA ceasefire in 1994. 'She is particularly good at the way in which the past constructs the present, how intense memories transfigure current experience . . .'. (*Independent on Sunday*) All her novels have been published by Faber.

JAYANTA MAHAPATRA 1928–

'. . . one must try somehow to reach the border between things understandable and ununderstandable in a poem, between life and death, between a straight line and a circle.' (Mahapatra, *Contemporary Poets*) He describes himself as being 'in love with silence' and sees a poem as being built out of the silence to which it must eventually return. 'He early developed a unique style in which multiplicity of significances, dislocated, often baffling syntax, and disruption of grammar are held together rather by rich patterns of imagery and sound than by any clarity of argument or narrative.' (Bruce King, *Contemporary Poets*) The London-based literary magazine, *Critical Quarterly*, was first to publish the poems of the physics lecturer, Jayanta Mahapatra (born in Cuttack, Orissa). He has since published many collections of poetry, and has been visiting writer/poet at various institutions in the US, Australia, Japan and the USSR. Has received the Jacob Glatstein memorial award, National Academy of Letters award and the Rockefeller Foundation award. Collections include *Close the Sky, Ten by Ten* (1971), *Waiting* (1979), *The False Start* (1980), *Relationship* (1980), *Life Signs* (1983), *Dispossessed Nests* (1986), *Burden of Waves and Fruit* (1988) and *Temple* (1989).

DEREK MAHON 1941–

The poem 'A Disused Shed in Co. Wexford', where a thousand fragile, forgotten mushrooms have lived and died in the unwatered dark, 'is now simply part of our culture's dialogue with itself, and that 'our' extends well beyond those who live in Ireland to include every individual conscious of the need to live something like an examined life in a dark time.' (Seamus Heaney, *Watching the River Flow*) Mahon was born and raised in the North. Educated in Trinity College, Dublin (overlapping with fellow northerner, Michael Longley). Has lived mainly outside Ireland since his graduation. His first volume of poetry, *Night-Crossing*, was published in 1968. This was followed by *Lives* (1972), *The Snow Party* (1975) and *The Hunt by Night* (1982). Other works include *The Hudson Letter* (1995) and *The Yellow Book* (1997). 'Mahon's poems are haunted by the good old bad times. The embattled stoicism of The Yellow Book includes as hero Austin Clarke, unlikely Sixties Belfast, Dublin and London, and a Swiftian misanthropy at full throttle.' (Gerald Dawe, *The Irish Times*) *Irish University Review* devoted an entire issue to his poetry in 1994.

EAMONN MALLIE 1950–

In their introduction to *The Fight For Peace: The Secret Story Behind The Irish Peace Process*, Mallie and McKittrick, two seasoned journalists, comment with astonishment on the successfully 'hidden labyrinth of secret contacts that lay beneath' the process of finding a peaceful solution to the crisis in Northern Ireland. It is a labyrinth that Mallie has been patiently exploring throughout his years as a political analyst. *The Provisional IRA* (with Bishop) was the first full-length study of the Provisional IRA, and was based partially on interviews with IRA activists. Born in South Armagh, Mallie went to school in Newry. After graduating from Trinity College, Dublin, he returned to the North and trained with BBC Northern Ireland as a Radio Current Affairs Producer. Appointed Downtown Radio's Political Correspondent, 1979. Set up his own private company, 'Eamonn Mallie News Services', 1990. He is political analyst on Northern Ireland for Channel 4 News and is currently researching a documentary for the Channel on The Good Friday Agreement. Northern Editor for Today FM, Dublin and Northern Ireland Correspondent for Agence France Presse. He writes a daily online 'Assembly in Focus', as well as news reports for Globalgateway Northern Ireland. Has written extensively on Irish art.

DAVID MALOUF 1934–

One of Australia's leading writers. Much of Malouf's work explores the settling of a continent – the different levels of unknown to be encountered, the creation of community, the exclusion from community. His paternal grandparents came to Australia from Lebanon in the 1880s, his maternal grandparents arrived from London on the eve of the First World War. He was born in Brisbane and graduated from the University of Queensland. He lived and worked in Europe from 1959 to 1968, returning to Australia to teach in the University of Sydney until 1977. Then, having published several volumes of poetry, including the highly-acclaimed *Bicycle and Other Poems* (1970) and *Neighbours in a Thicket* (1974), as well as his first novel, *Johnno*, he decided to devote himself to writing full-time, dividing his time between Italy and Australia. His second novel, *An Imaginary Life* (1978), is 'virtually a prose poem of great lyric power.' (Thomas Shapcott, *Contemporary Poets*) *The Great World* won the Commonwealth Writers' Prize and the Prix Femina Étranger in 1991, while *Remembering Babylon* won the inaugural IMPAC Dublin Literary Award (1996). Has written three opera librettos, one an adaptation of Patrick White's novel, *Voss. The Conversations at Curlow Creek* appeared in 1996.

MARY MANNING 1906–

'"I understand it's to commemorate the tercentenary of Tomas O'Sullivan's birth."/"And who was Tomas O'Sullivan?" asked her ladyship haughtily./ "He was a great Irish poet born here, my dear; he was blind and wandered all over Ireland reciting his poetry."/"They wander all over America now," said Albie brightly; she kept up with the times to a certain extent. "Rubber, isn't it?"' (Ballyfungus's impending Poetry Festival comes under discussion at the bridge table in the Ferncourt drawing room, *The Last Chronicles of Ballyfungus*, 1978.) Manning's first play, *Youth's the Season ———?* (1931), written while she was still in her twenties, has been described by Brian Fallon as 'one of the most striking first plays of the 1930s'. Born in Dublin. Studied art in London and Boston. Worked for the Gate as publicity manager and editor of *Motley*, the theatre's magazine. Moved to Boston in the mid 1930s and was one of the founders of the Cambridge Poets' Theatre. Returned to Ireland after her first husband's death. Theatre critic for *Hibernia* during 1970s. Her 'comic but moving' (*Dictionary of Irish Literature*) adaptation of Frank O'Connor's novel, *The Saint and Mary Kate*, was performed in the Abbey (1968). Returned to the US in 1979.

DAVID MARCUS 1924–

' . . . The apogee of this generous patronage came some years later when David Marcus founded *New Irish Writing*. Every Saturday a whole page of the *Irish Press* was devoted to prose and poetry hot off the typewriter. It seemed important that imaginative writing was being published in a newspaper rather than in the *cordon sanitaire* of a literary magazine. Marcus's acute, expansive editorship brought together young writers from all over Ireland and educated them about each other.' (Michael Longley, *Watching the River Flow*) Before initiating the deeply influential *New Irish Writing* in 1968, Marcus had practised as a barrister for several years. A Cork man, he graduated from University College, Cork. His first serious involvement with literature was as founder and editor of the two journals, *Irish Writing* (1946–54) and *Poetry Ireland*. He has been an enormous encouragement to aspiring and established Irish writers over several decades and has never lost his dedication to literature. He has edited many anthologies of short stories, and is himself a novelist, producing an early novel *To Next Year in Jerusalem* (1954), *A Land Not Theirs* (1986) and *A Land in Flames* (1987).

AUGUSTINE MARTIN 1935–1995

Professor of Anglo-Irish Literature and Drama at University College, Dublin from 1979 until the year of his death. One of his most enduring legacies to Irish literature was the successful retrieval of the Patrick Kavanagh archives from America. They are now held by UCD. Deeply involved in the practical preservation and on-going vitality of Ireland's literary heritage, he directed the Yeats Summer School (1978–81), represented the National University of Ireland in Seanad Éireann (1973–81), served on the board of the Abbey Theatre and founded the James Joyce Summer School in 1987. While still a teacher in Roscrea (1958–65) he co-founded the Association of Teachers of English to reform the syllabus. He subsequently devised and presented a series of educational programmes for Telefís Scoile. His lecturing qualities were much appreciated by his own students, and he was also much in demand abroad, lecturing in North America, Europe, the Lebanon, India, Japan and Singapore. He published both critical studies and school textbooks. *Bearing Witness: Essays on Anglo Irish Literature* is a selection of his work over three decades.

'McCabe is recognised as a highly-gifted if reluctant writer.' (*Field Day Anthology*) His outstanding play is *The King of the Castle* (1964) which won an *Irish Life* Award. It describes the efforts of the locally powerful (but sexually impotent) Scober, to hire a man to impregnate his wife. As with all such powerful and disturbing plays, it was controversial. 'I'm very glad I wrote it. Even though at the time it was disembowelled as a dirty play.' (McCabe to Eileen Battersby, *The Irish Times*) His next major success was in the 1970s with the three-part television drama on Northern Ireland – *Victims*. Adapted Thomas Flanagan's *The Year of the French* for RTÉ/Channel 4. *Death and Nightingales*, a hauntingly painful novel of love and betrayal set in the latter half of the nineteenth century, appeared in 1992. 'His honest style and unflinching confrontation of the violence inherent in the Irish character provide a refreshing antidote to the marketable charm of much Irish writing.' (Christopher Murray, *Dictionary of Irish Literature*) *Tales from the Poorhouse* was recently adapted in English and Irish for television. Born in Glasgow. His family moved back to Ireland at the beginning of the war. Graduated from University College, Cork. Has farmed in County Monaghan for many years.

'I always used to wonder how you could meet a guy in a bar that had you enthralled talking in the vernacular and yet when you go to read a novel you don't find any of it at all. You're suddenly into this detached stuff and I never was comfortable with that.' (McCabe to John Kelly, *The Irish Times*) There is nothing detached about McCabe's language. No author stands between you and Francie Brady. You start reading *The Butcher Boy* (successfully filmed by Neil Jordan) and it's not that he's in your head. You are in Francie Brady's head and you can't get out. McCabe could have been lost to literature had he followed his other love – music. 'I was playing with Paddy Hanrahan and the Oklahoma Showband – haring round the country and teaching at the same time. And I kind of weighed up the way showband men lived at that time . . . And so I thought to myself: well, it's going to be a toss up between this and writing. And if it's going to be writing I just can't live at this pace.' (McCabe to Kelly) Other works include *The Dead School* and *Breakfast on Pluto*.

'I discovered, early on, that I'd never be able to write a front page story . . . I discovered this particularly on Bloody Sunday in Derry, when I was lying on the street while people around me got shot dead . . . My version appeared on the inside pages. I wrote about how the rest of us felt, lying on the ground.' (McCafferty, introducing *The Best of Nell*, 1984) Derry-born feminist and nationalist, 'born to be an eyewitness'. (Eavan Boland) Graduated from Queen's University, Belfast, travelled extensively, worked in a kibbutz and returned to Derry in 1968. Joined the Civil Rights movement. Was a columnist for *The Irish Times* during the 1970s. 'In the Eyes of the Law' highlighted the inadequacies of the legal system as a tool of justice. Contributing editor, *MS* magazine, TV critic for the *Sunday Tribune*, and columnist for *Hot Press*. Currently a columnist for the *Sunday Tribune*. 'Nell McCafferty has increased the oxygen in this community. Because of the questions she has asked, the answers she has punctured, there is that bit more space, more ease, more manoeuvre.' (Eavan Boland, prefacing *The Best of Nell*) Other works include *A Woman to Blame: The Kerry Babies Case*, *Goodnight Sisters* and *Peggy Deery*.

'It's funny, you spend four years writing a book and then it's done and you've said what you wanted to say, you know what you meant. But you can't tell anyone else what it means, because now it's their book and things will mean different things to different people' – McCann to Eileen Battersby (*The Irish Times*) on the publication of *This Side of Brightness* (1998). McCann was born in Dublin. He has lived in America, Japan and Ireland and divides his time between Dublin and New York City. *Fishing the Sloe Black River*, a collection of short stories set in Ireland and America, won the 1994 Rooney Prize for Irish Literature and he was hailed as a major new voice. Other works include his first novel, *Songdogs*, and *This Side of Brightness* (set both physically and emotionally below the surface of New York) one of the seven books shortlisted for the £100,000 International IMPAC Dublin Literary Award this year. His new book, *Everything in This Country Must,* a novella and two stories, has just been published. Earlier this year he began a new novel, which 'starts in Russia in the 1940s, and is about a male dancer'. (McCann to *The Irish Times*)

'We have the keenly perceptive chronicles of Thomas McCarthy, in which the thwarted ideals and misplaced hopes of the new Irish Republic are scrutinised and exposed in the hope, I assume, that some of this burdensome inheritance can be abandoned.' (Cathal Ó Searcaigh, *Watching the River Flow*) Novelist as well as poet, McCarthy has used both literary forms to pursue his scrutiny of the political and personal. His first poetry collection, *The First Convention*, won the Patrick Kavanagh Award in 1977. From Waterford, McCarthy has lived in Cork (where he went to college) since the 1970s. Works in the Cork City Library. Current editor of *The Cork Review*. A fellow of the International Writing Program at the University of Iowa 1978–1979. Awarded Irish-American Foundation's Literary Award, 1984, and the O'Shaughnessy Poetry Prize of the Irish-American Cultural Institute, 1991. Former editor of *Poetry Ireland Review*. His two novels, *Without Power* and *Aysa and Christine*, were published in 1991 and 1992. Other works include *Gardens of Remembrance* (1998) and *Mr Dineen's Careful Parade: New and Selected Poems* (1999), 'one of the more secure achievements of recent southern poetry.' (Patrick Crotty, *The Irish Times*)

'It was a sight that rooted them [the foxes] to the spot. All they could do was stand and stare, wide-eyed, open-mouthed and unbelieving. The model in the centre was dressed in a coat of fox furs, and around her neck she wore a complete fox skin. The legs hung limply from her shoulders, and a fine head that once was cunning and free was clasped lifeless across the base of the tail.' (*Run with the Wind*) McCaughren has written a series of six gripping stories of foxes fighting for their survival against the depredations of man. In a note at the back of *Run with the Wind*, McCaughren tells us that during the single season of 1981–82, 40,700 fox pelts were exported from Ireland. Fortunately, the prices for pelts began to drop in 1982 and an increase in fox numbers was reported. From Ballymena in Northern Ireland, McCaughren lives and works in Dublin. He is a broadcaster with RTÉ, and has written numerous books for children. They have been translated into seven languages, including Latvian, and his awards include the Bisto/Children's Book Trust Book of the Decade 1980–1990 and the White Raven International Youth Library Citation.

'Nevertheless, a bad heart is a bad heart and no matter how well intentioned it is or whether it is in the right place or not, given time, one way or another, it will kill you.' So broods Crowe, strange protagonist of *Crowe's Requiem*, the Galway-based novel with its wonderfully gothic first chapters, which was published in 1998 by Jonathan Cape. McCormack's first book, *Getting it in the Head,* is a collection of widely-praised short stories (macabre and blackly humorous) which won the Rooney Prize when it was published in 1996. 'When it comes to graphic description of dismemberment, it is clear he learned a lot from a time as a butcher's assistant.' (Eileen Battersby, *The Irish Times*) He grew up in County Mayo. Abandoned his first attempt at third level education (electronic engineering) after a year, but following a period as a gardener he returned to study English and philosophy. Graduated from NUI, Galway, but a thesis on Heidegger fell victim to his fiction. Was one of five novelists short-listed for the major Kerry Ingredients Book of the Year Award at Listowel Writers Week in 1999. (Won posthumously by J.M. O'Neill.) McCormack lives in the west of Ireland.

'When I look back on my childhood I wonder how I survived at all. It was, of course, a miserable childhood: the happy childhood is hardly worth your while. Worse than the ordinary miserable childhood is the miserable Irish childhood, and worse yet is the miserable Irish Catholic childhood.' Undoubtedly the most quoted paragraph in *Angela's Ashes*, '[t]hrusting comedy into the very teeth of misery' (Julian Moynahan, *The New York Review of Books*), it sets the self-mocking tone which prevents any pathos from creeping into the story of Frank McCourt's impression of a childhood spent mainly in the Limerick slums of the 1940s. '[T]he construction of the slowly maturing child narrator is the central imaginative achievement of the book.' (Moynahan) Although his book was not unanimously welcomed in Limerick, the city as a whole sees its tourism industry as benefiting enormously from the publicity engendered both by the book and by Alan Parker's film. *Angela's Ashes*, published in 1996, has sold more than five million copies and has been translated into twenty languages. 'His reading of it on audio tape . . . is the best reason I can think of for taking a long car journey.' (John Boland, *The Irish Times*) The sequel, '*Tis*, describes his adult life in the US.

When Fermanagh teacher, historian and broadcaster Breege McCusker began teaching at St. Mary's College in Irvinestown in 1969, she found that there were no local sources for her students. So she produced them herself, mindful that she didn't want 'young people to feel the rage that I had as a youngster when I read some local work which was so obviously biased against one section of the community.' As a result of her '[h]onest reporting for a general readership' she has found herself 'accepted in all communities.' She became interested in local history as a child, through listening to local conversations in her mother's public house in Irvinestown. Publications include *Fermanagh: Land of Lake and Legend*, *Irvinestown through the Years*, *Castle Archdale and Fermanagh in World War II*, *Necarne Castle and the Ulster Lakeland Equestrian Park* and *Lowtherstown Workhouse*. She has also made several videos, including *Devenish Island: a Monastic Settlement*, *Jack Carrothers – a Soldier of the Great War* and *Bridging the Centuries in North Fermanagh*. She is Fermanagh contributor to BBC Radio Ulster, 'Your Place and Mine', presenter of Lakeland Radio and Outreach Officer for the Public Records Office for Northern Ireland.

'I think Martin's voice is unique; he's a young Londoner of Irish parents and he is writing plays set in the west of Ireland. This is the world of his imagination; it is a world he is creating entirely out of his imagination, stimulated by Ireland. It is a modern sensibility.' (Garry Hynes to Eileen Battersby, *The Irish Times*) McDonagh is the creator of the brutally funny, brutally painful *The Beauty Queen of Leenane* (first of *The Leenane Trilogy – A Skull in Connemara* and *The Lonesome West* being the other two) which took New York by storm in 1998, winning four Tony Awards. 'The 1950s is laid over the 1990s, giving the play's apparent realism the ghostly, dizzying feeling of a superimposed photograph.' (Fintan O'Toole) *The Cripple of Inishmaan*, first of *The Aran* trilogy, opened in New York in the same year. *The Leenane Trilogy* was staged in its entirety by Druid in 1997. 'For over six hours . . . the audience had not only survived but also enjoyed one of the whitest knuckle roller coaster rides ever to career across an Irish stage . . . ' . (Jocelyn Clarke, *The Sunday Tribune*)

McDonnell's first novel, *The Broken Commandment*, was shortlisted for the Guinness Peat Aviation Award in 1989. Although the novel did not win the main award (which went to John Banville for *The Book of Evidence*), it so impressed novelist Graham Greene that a special prize, the Guinness Peat First Fiction Award, was created to acknowledge the strength of his opinion. McDonnell's writing apprenticeship had started long before. In 1978 he was winner of the *Ireland's Own* short-story competition. He published several stories in that magazine and in 1984 his short story, 'Old Father Time', was broadcast on LBC, an independent London radio station. Many short stories have followed. Since his 1989 success, McDonnell has published a further novel, *Imagination of the Heart*. He has also written four books for children – *The Boy Who Saved Christmas*, and its sequel, *Can Timmy Save Toyland?*, *Children of Stone* (set in the Stone Age) and *The Knock Airport Mystery* (a fast-paced hi-jacking mystery for older children). Born in County Mayo (within a couple of miles of Knock Airport's runway), McDonnell lived in London for many years, working as a service engineer. Recently spent two terms as writer-in-residence for County Limerick.

'McGahern's economy is not merely structural; his telling observations and circumstantialities have a quick poetic precision that helps establish the characteristic bitter-sweetness of his vision.' (Field Day Anthology) Father a senior police officer. Raised in County Roscommon. Went to University College, Dublin. While a primary school teacher in Dublin, he published his first novel, *The Barracks* (1963), and was awarded the AE Memorial Award. His hugely controversial second novel, *The Dark* (1965), was banned. His teaching contract was not renewed and he left the country for a decade. He has been visiting professor throughout the US. Awarded Honorary D.Litt. from Trinity College, Dublin. Other works include *The Leavetaking* (1974), *The Pornographer* (1979) and *Amongst Women* (1990), another compelling story of paternal dominance (short-listed for the Booker Prize and later adapted for television). Received GPA Award in 1992 and Le Prix Étranger Écureuil in 1994. 'In all of McGahern's fiction the claustrophobic, behind-closed-doors world of family life is intense and psychologically both complex and volatile. It is also both isolated and self-isolating . . . ' (Hunt Mahony, *Contemporary Irish Literature*) Short stories include *Nightlines* (1970), *Getting Through* (1978), *High Ground* (1985) and *Collected Stories* (1992).

MEDBH MCGUCKIAN 1950–

'Her poems revel in their imaginative and elaborate qualities. It is not just a matter of dense imagery and difficult metaphor. Meaning is constantly deferred; sometimes, by a careful twist, the meaning is placed out of reach *after* the reader thinks it has been grasped.' (R.J.C. Watt, *Contemporary Poets*) Critics have found the opacity of her poetry unsettling, but most have succumbed to the 'protean quality of McGuckian's attractiveness'. (Mary O'Connor, *Modern Irish Writers*) Born in Belfast, she attended Queen's University where she was taught by Seamus Heaney, an early mentor. Her teaching has included a period as visiting lecturer at the University of California, Berkeley. She was the first female writer-in-residence at Queen's University. Writer-in-residence at the University of Ulster, Coleraine, 1995. Her works include *The Flower Master*, the title of which 'suggests a nearly Victorian substitution of flora for the human fauna in the recurring sexual or sensual encounters portrayed here' (Hunt Mahony, *Contemporary Irish Literature*), *Venus and the Rain*, *On Ballycastle Beach*, *Marconi's Cottage,* and *Captain Lavender*. *Selected Poems* was shortlisted for *The Irish Times* Irish Literature: Poetry Prize in 1999. She has received many awards and has been widely anthologised.

FRANK MCGUINNESS 1953–

'It was an eye-opener for a Catholic Republican, as I am, to have to examine the complexity, diversity, disturbance and integrity of the other side, the Protestant people.' – McGuinness describing the research and writing of his most widely-known play, *Observe the Sons of Ulster Marching Towards the Somme*, originally directed by Patrick Mason. From Buncrana, Donegal, McGuinness set his first play, *The Factory Girls*, in the locality. Based on the experiences of hostages captured in Beirut and held over several years, the play, *Someone Who'll Watch Over Me* (Hampstead, West End and Broadway), depicts the extraordinary relationship which builds up between three men of different nationalities (Irish, British and American) chained to a wall in a cell. The retention of humanity and the dispelling of despair are achieved through a variety of means, most memorably through bouts of savagely riotous humour and the telling of stories. Other plays include *Mutabilitie*, *Baglady*, *Innocence* and *Carthaginians*. '*Carthaginians* is my elegy to the dead and the living of Derry, the living who kept going, in Dido's words, "Surviving. Carthage has not been destroyed."' Translations include *Hedda Gabler* and *A Doll's House* (which won four Tony Awards in 1997).

TOM MACINTYRE 1933–

In the 1980s, experimental playwright Tom MacIntyre, director Patrick Mason and actor Tom Hickey collaborated closely in the production of several plays, most notably *The Great Hunger* (an adaptation of Kavanagh's poem). More physical than verbal, it was critically well received and went on to tour the UK, France, Russia and the USA. *The Bearded Lady* (1984) was an 'irreverent but probing play that explores the contradictory personality of Jonathan Swift through sexual means.' (Christina Hunt Mahony, *Contemporary Irish Literature*) *Good Evening, Mr. Collins*, 'more conventionally scripted than many of MacIntyre's works' (Hunt Mahony), was a highly individual portrait of Michael Collins. MacIntyre is from County Cavan. Graduated from University College, Dublin. Taught at Clongowes Wood. Has taught creative writing at the University of Michigan and Williams College in Massachusetts. Other plays include *Rise Up, Lovely Sweeney* (1985), *Dance for Your Daddy* (1987), *Kitty O'Shea* (1990), *Chickadee* (1990) and *Sheep's Milk on the Boil* (1994). Has also published a novel and three poetry collections. In 1999 he received the BBC Northern Ireland's Irish Language Drama Award for the Peacock Theatre's production of his play, *Caoineadh Árt Ui Laoghaire*.

SIOBHÁN MCKENNA 1923–1986

'"Oh, my grief, I've lost him surely, I've lost the only playboy of the western world" Siobhán uttered this lament in a voice lowered to a whisper of infinite longing, the perfect coda to a performance of sinuous sensuality.' (Micheál Ó hAodha, *Siobhán: A Memoir of an Actress*) McKenna came to international prominence as Pegeen Mike in Synge's *Playboy of the Western World* at the Edinburgh Theatre Festival in 1951. Her name was to be linked to the role throughout her life. Born in Belfast, but grew up in Galway. Began her acting career in 1940 with Galway's Irish-language theatre company, An Taibhdhearc, before joining the Abbey in 1944. Played role of St. Joan both in her own Irish translation of Shaw's *Saint Joan* (in 1951) and in English ('the richest portrait of saintliness since Falconetti shaved her head for Dreyer's film *La Passion de Jeanne d'Arc*' – Kenneth Tynan, quoted in Ó hAodha). Other outstanding roles were as Juno in O'Casey's *Juno and the Paycock* and Josie in Eugene O'Neill's *Moon for the Misbegotten*. Her Molly Bloom soliloquy from Joyce's *Ulysses* was the highlight of her one-woman presentation, *Here Are Ladies*. One of her last great theatre roles was in the Druid production of Tom Murphy's *Bailegangaire*.

PAULA MEEHAN 1955–

'My recurring obsessions are about class, about the different levels of access and opportunity people have. People who know me well would say I'm working out parts of my own story in the characters in *Cell*.' (Meehan, talking to Rosita Boland, *The Irish Times*, about the play based on her experiences as writer-in-residence in Mountjoy and other prisons) Meehan is both poet and playwright. A Dubliner from Finglas. Studied at Trinity College, Dublin and at Eastern Washington University. Writer-in-residence in Trinity and Mountjoy at the same time and found a marked similarity in the responses of participants from both institutions to material presented to them. *The Man who was Marked by Winter* (1991) was shortlisted for the *Irish Times*/Aer Lingus Irish Literature Prize for Poetry. A 'major female voice from the 90s . . . her poem "The Pattern" has already taken on the status of a classic. A richly textured evocation of a childhood growing up in Dublin's inner city and the deeply ambiguous relationship between mother and daughter are explored throughout the poem . . .' . (Nuala Ní Dhomhnaill, *Watching the River Flow*) A fifth collection of poetry is due this year.

M.J. MOLLOY 1917–1994

'In all of Molloy's plays there is nostalgia for a time when men had a proper regard for each other and for the land, a time when depopulation had not reduced rural Ireland to a gaggle of testy and self-righteous bachelors, a time before technology and an unscrupulous middle class purloined the land.' (Arthur McGuinness, *Contemporary Dramatists*) Molloy lived in County Galway virtually throughout his life. A folk-dramatist, he has been compared to Synge. But, as Robert O'Driscoll comments in his introduction to Molloy's plays, there is an essential difference between them '. . . Synge was an outsider trying to get in. Molloy, on the other hand, is an insider getting out.' Molloy wrote about his own world, re-imagined and enriched through his explorations of the folklore, the social history, tempered by his awareness of rural depopulation and continuing social change. 'All of my plays are a protest against the cruel, unromantic, mechanistic mentality of modern times.' (Molloy to O'Driscoll) Molloy spent four years in a seminary. He began writing plays during a long struggle with bone tuberculosis. Farmed from 1950 to 1972. His plays include *The King of Friday's Men*, *The Visiting House* and *The Wood of the Whispering* (revived by Druid in 1983).

JOHN MONTAGUE 1929–

Currently first Ireland Professor of Poetry. Born Brooklyn, New York, but spent his childhood with paternal relatives in Armagh, separated from his parents and siblings. '. . . my effort to understand as much of the modern world as possible serves only to illuminate the destruction of that small area from which I initially came, and that theme in turn is only part of the larger one of continually threatened love. All of us are uprooted now, subject to the seismic waves of the late 20th century; we must warn and warm ourselves against a new ice age.' (Montague in *Contemporary Poets*) A poet who can meticulously describe possession – of love, of place, of language – and its loss. Attended University College, Dublin, Yale and University of Iowa. Was Paris correspondent for *The Irish Times*. Lectured in University College, Cork, 1972–88. 'I have three countries; two Irelands, North and South. Then there's America, where I was born and France, where you can be an intellectual.' (Montague to Eileen Battersby, *The Irish Times*) *Collected Poems* (1995) seen by Bernard O'Donoghue (*Poetry Ireland Review*) as endorsing the claim of the editors that 'it has the look of a masterpiece'. Recently published *Smashing the Piano*.

BRIAN MOORE 1921–1999

Confounded people throughout his writing career by continually moving on. 'Every three years or so, he reinvented himself by writing an entirely different novel. People say the novel is dead but the novel will never be dead because people love stories. And Brian Moore was a master at bringing readers into a story.' (Dermot Bolger to Rosita Boland, *The Irish Times*) Most commentators agree that his first book, *The Lonely Passion of Judith Hearne*, was the most outstanding of his brilliantly kaleidoscopic collection of novels. He never allowed himself to be impeded by that verdict. Amongst succeeding novels are *The Emperor of Icecream*, *The Temptation of Eileen Hughes*, *Black Robe* and *Lies of Silence*, which, though short-listed for the Booker Prize in 1990, caused confusion for critics. 'The combination of an exciting plot with a crisis-ridden central hero is not enough to stop *Lies of Silence* … from being at times too close to the border line of an unthinking type of popular fiction.' (Colin Graham, *Contemporary Novelists*) But the same critic ends by admitting that the book's 'fascination with moral dilemmas and how they illustrate, determine, and shape the personality of the individual is typical of the best of Moore's writing.' Born in Belfast, Moore spent most of his adult life in Canada and the US.

CHRISTY MOORE 1945–

From County Kildare, Moore formed The Rakes of Kildare with Donal Lunny in the 1960s. Worked briefly in a bank. The bank strike of 1966 afforded him the opportunity to tour folk clubs in England. Dominic Behan produced Moore's first album, *Paddy on the Road*. Returning to Ireland, he released *Prosperous* and formed the band Planxty with Liam O'Flynn, Donal Lunny and Andy Irvine. After Planxty's final break-up and the demise of Moore and Lunny's Moving Hearts, Moore went solo. He is a very physical, intense performer. 'Pointed, humorous, and occasionally scabrous, Moore's songs . . . are reminders of the art of protest through song.' (Tony Clayton-Lea, *The Irish Times*) Had to retire for health reasons, but has recently made a 'positive and life-affirming' (Joe Jackson, *The Irish Times*) album, *Traveller*, and is preparing an autobiography for publication. His manager, Mattie Fox, thinks that 'rarely has the dynamism of his public performance been captured on wax or tape . . . The clinical nature of a studio setting has always got in the way of Christy expressing himself the way he can in a live performance.' (*The Irish Times*) Has recorded many albums, including *The Iron Behind the Velvet*, *Unfinished Revolution*, *Graffiti Tongue*.

PAUL MULDOON 1951–

'I have this poem pinned up beside my writing desk. I am deeply envious of it. So much so that every time I look up it spurs me on to try again . . . In its extraordinary technical virtuosity and depth of heart it sums up everything that I consider valuable in Irish poetry in the 90s.' (Nuala Ní Dhomhnaill on selecting the poem 'Long Finish' for *Watching the River Flow*) Muldoon, seen as one of the most exciting poets writing in the English language, was elected to the five-year position of Oxford Professor of Poetry in 1999, a position once held by Seamus Heaney. Born in County Armagh. His father was a gardener and mushroom farmer, his mother a schoolteacher. Lives in New Jersey. Christina Hunt Mahony describes him as 'acquiring an American crossover reputation that is quite unusual among recent Irish writers.' His works, packed with a fast-moving Joycean absurdity and depth, include *New Weather*, *Mules*, *Why Brownlee Left*, *Quoof*, *Meeting the British*, *Madoc: A Mystery*. Won the TS Eliot Memorial Prize, and, in 1997, the Irish Times Irish Literature Prize for *New Selected Poems 1968–94*.

MICHAEL MULLEN 1937–

Mullen's writing comes from 'an urgency to define the inscape and the landscape'. From Castlebar, County Mayo, he graduated from University College, Dublin, 'where literature was taught as biology'. *Kelly*, which he was encouraged to write by David Marcus ('most unusual and worthy'), was published in 1981. His books fall into various categories. *Kelly* and *Festival of Fools* are mythology. His trilogy, *The Hungry Land*, *Rites of Inheritance*, *The House of Mirrors* are Irish historical novels. Others, such as *The Midnight Country*, *Pillars of Fire*, *The Last Days of the Romanovs* and *An Bóthar Fada*, deal with some of the great themes of European history. Mullen is also an outstanding author of historical fiction for teenagers and children, moving outside Ireland to introduce children to the wider historical field. 'I deal with essential historical problems using original sources.' Other titles include *To Hell or Connaught*, *The Sea Wolves from the North*, *The Flight of the Earls*, *The Long March* and *The Four Masters*. He also writes in Irish and having just completed a large novel, *Díoltas*, he plans an Irish-language sequence of four Connaught-based historical novels spanning the twentieth century.

DERVLA MURPHY 1931–

Wrote her first travel book, *Full Tilt*, in 1965, but has been travelling physically and mentally all her life. *Wheels within Wheels* describes her County Waterford childhood and early adult life curtailed by the debilitating illness of her mother. The ability to examine herself so honestly underlies her ability to observe the lives of others. Talking to Eileen Battersby (*The Irish Times*) about *South From the Limpopo* in 1997, she said: 'I was pretty shattered. I thought I could understand the dynamics of the place – I've read Brink and Gordimer, Coeztee, Brytenbach . . . I can honestly say I have been reading about it for 40 years. I was so wrong.' By 1968 she had cycled in India, travelled to Nepal and explored the Ethiopian highlands on foot. The birth of her daughter in 1968 was no deterrent. In 1973 they set off together through South India. Together they have traversed such diverse areas – on foot, by pony, with pack-mules – as the Peruvian Andes and Cameroon, West Africa. In 1978 she turned her attention to Northern Ireland and *A Place Apart* resulted. Other books include *Tales from Two Cities* (1987), *The Ukimwi Road* (1993), *Visiting Rwanda* (1998) and *One Foot in Laos* (1999).

JOHN MURPHY 1924–1998

Murphy's only produced play, *The Country Boy* (in which a returned emigrant attempts to prevent his younger brother from repeating his own mistakes), was first performed by the Group Theatre company in Belfast (1959) and, a month later, by the Abbey. 'It ought to have been the beginning of an extraordinary theatrical career. Ironically, though, John Murphy was so much a part of the world he described that he was subject to the same farces he conjured up in the play. He could not find a place in the Ireland he knew so well.' (Fintan O'Toole) His second play, *The Man from Ballybeg*, was ignored. Always popular with amateur drama groups, *The Country Boy* was produced professionally at Dublin's Andrews Lane Theatre in 1995 and again, last summer, by Druid. 'It wins because, while the simplicities may be of their time, the 1960s, the emotions are true and lasting. As realised here [Druid] in some outstanding performances, they pack an empathetic wallop that brings a lump to the throat and moisture to the eye.' (Gerry Colgan, *The Irish Times*) From Charlestown, County Mayo, Murphy worked as a ships engineer in Belfast (where he wrote *The Country Boy*) before emigrating to America, where he worked in the Hollywood studios.

RICHARD MURPHY 1927–

'His poems will often feature a word excavated lovingly from the lexicon. The word is then presented for exhibition, demanding our concentration and unstinting admiration. Words like "grapnel," "dewlap," "schist," . . . and "unvermiculated" challenge and astound the reader new to Murphy.' (Hunt Mahony, *Contemporary Irish Literature*) Born in County Mayo, but educated in England. Of Anglo-Irish background, a 'crucial impetus' in Murphy's work has been 'a willed bridging of two traditions, an effort to connect sensuously and emotionally with two versions of Irish history.' (Thomas McCarthy, *Contemporary Poets*) His first collection, *Sailing to an Island,* was a lyrical engagement with the west coast of Ireland, his own terrain. *The Battle of Aughrim* tackled the Irish defeat in the Jacobean wars and its continuing reverberations in the 1960s. ('Murphy underscores the irony, though his case is not unique, of having had forebears fighting on both sides of the battle' – Hunt Mahony.) *The Price of Stone* is a sonnet sequence in which buildings become the narrators. 'He is one of our least celebrated poets, which is a pity, because he is one the very few who matter.' (John Boland, *The Irish Times*) His collected poems are due to be published this year.

TOM MURPHY 1935–

In conversation with Pat McCabe at the 1999 Cúirt in Galway, Tuam-born Murphy confessed he didn't know how to write a play. The author of such acclaimed plays as *A Whistle in the Dark*, *Famine*, *The Gigli Concert*, *Conversations on a Homecoming*, *Bailegangaire* and *The House* was describing the impossibility of reducing the process of writing anything to a step-by-step guide to success. Emotion, both writers agreed, was the root without which nothing else could happen. *A Whistle in the Dark*, rejected by the Abbey (Irish people do not behave that way), was first staged in London in 1961 to a mixture of acclaim and controversy. It took the 1968 production of *Famine* in the Peacock Theatre to establish his reputation in Ireland. One of his most fruitful periods as a playwright came during his association with Garry Hynes and the Druid Theatre when both *Conversations on a Homecoming* and *Bailegangaire* (with Siobhan McKenna as Mommo) were produced for the first time. And now *The House* – 'one of his most gripping and enlightening . . . set in 1950s Ireland and there is no trace of nostalgia in it. It may be the most compelling indictment of emigration ever committed to the stage . . .'. (David Nolan, *The Irish Times*)

LES MURRAY 1938–

' . . . the language of poetry is never absolute or unique. Part of its fascination . . . is the way in which it can disclose endless new variations of its own ancient possibilities. That can happen when it becomes the instrument of a poet who is as unafraid of its old sly echoes and duplicities as Les Murray has always been.' (John Bayley, reviewing *Subhuman Redneck Poems* in *The New York Review of Books*) Raised on a farm (to which he returned in 1985) in New South Wales, Australia. Graduated from the University of Sydney and worked as a translator before turning to full-time writing. Co-edited *Poetry Australia* and in 1991 became literary editor of *Quadrant*. Edited *The New Oxford Book of Australian Verse* and *The Anthology of Australian Religious Verse*. 'He simultaneously displays reverence for the Bushland, Aborigines, and Aboriginal culture; respect for pioneers like his own ancestors . . . and admiration for what has become the characteristic Australian temperament . . . '. (*Norton Anthology of Poetry*) Other works include *Ethnic Radio*, *The Boys Who Stole the Funeral*, *Dog Fox Field*, *The Rabbiter's Bounty*, *The Paperbark Tree* and *Translations from the Natural World*.

'There is something second sighted, as it were, about Ní Chuilleanáin's work, by which I don't mean that she has any prophetic afflatus, more that her poems see things anew, in a rinsed and dreamstruck light. They are at once as plain as an anecdote told on the doorstep and as haunting as a soothsayer's greetings.' (Seamus Heaney, *Watching the River Flow*) Born in Cork where her father was Professor of Irish. Her mother was Eilís Dillon, the novelist. Studied at University College, Cork and Oxford. She is a Fellow of Trinity College, Dublin where she has lectured in English since 1966, the year in which she won the *Irish Times* poetry award. Commentators note her obsession with water, myth and legend. Her first collection, *Acts and Monuments* (1972), won the Patrick Kavanagh Award. In 1975 she was a joint founder of *Cyphers*, a literary journal. She remains an editor. Received the O'Shaughnessy Award of the Irish-American Cultural Institute in 1992. Other collections include *Site of Ambush* (1975), *The Second Voyage* (1977), *The Rose Geranium* (1981), *The Magdalene Sermon* (1989), which was short-listed for the *Irish Times*/Aer Lingus Award, and *The Brazen Serpent* (1994). She is currently working on a new collection.

Ní Dhomhnaill recently described how after several years of carrying out her life under the influence of *Portrait of the Artist as a Young Man,* she realised that '[i]f I had to be living in a book, the book I should have been living in was one which until that time was unavailable to me because of the Censorship of Publications Act. That book was Kate O'Brien's wonderful *Land of Spices*, set in the very boarding school that I had gone to myself. Unlike Joyce's bildungsroman which calls on the hero to cut and run, the plot of this book entails the opposite movement, a moving out of frigid loneliness into warmth and human entanglement.' (*The Irish Times*) Writing in Irish and brilliantly served by translators, her poetry richly, sensually and teasingly displays all the diversity of human entanglement. She shows us still using myth to explain ourselves, excuse ourselves, enrich ourselves. Although born in England, her roots lie in the Dingle Gaeltacht and by choosing to write in Irish, she uses the entanglement of language to add further layers of intricacy to her poetry. Graduated from University College, Cork and spent some years in Turkey. Works include the bilingual editions *Pharoah's Daughter*, *The Astrakan Coat* and *The Water Horse* (containing a selection from the prize-winning *Feis* and *Cead Aighnis*).

'The people sent out from Clare went from one edge of the world to the other edge of the world. I sometimes wonder if built into me there's a funny kind of memory of this edge to edge.' (*The Sunday Tribune*, quoted by Pat Sheeran, *The Book of the Burren*) Of Irish descent, Nolan was described by Sir Kenneth Clark as 'Australia's only real painter'. Attended the National Gallery of Victoria School. Later studied engraving and lithography at Atelier 17 in Paris. Began as an abstract painter, influenced by Klee and Lázló Moholy-Nagy. Grew more representational as he became more engrossed with the historical and legendary figures of the Australian landscape (a particular fascination was the bushranger, Ned Kelly) and the landscape itself. Was associated with the avant-garde journal, *Angry Penguins*. Moved to England in 1950. Designed stage-sets for ballet and opera, including Kenneth MacMillan's version of *The Rite of Spring* (Covent Garden, 1962). His first solo exhibition was in 1940. In 1949 his work was exhibited in Paris and in 1951 he had his first solo exhibition in London. He donated his Gallipoli paintings to the Australian War Memorial in Canberra in 1974. Knighted in 1981. In 1986 he presented fifty of his paintings to the Irish people.

As Joe Noonan says himself, 'As a postman – for over twenty years – I have travelled the byways and boreens around Lough Graney. In fact it was only when I became a postman that I realised how little I knew about the parish in which I lived and more importantly about the people and interesting characters that lived around me. I've had twenty years observing, twenty years conversing, and twenty years of learning.' He is the postman in Flagmount near Feakle, County Clare. He has compiled, written, illustrated and published two books of poetry, *Songs & Recitations*, and *Songs, Recitations & Short Stories*. The books are a labour of love and a tangible result of community spirit engendered by the dynamism of a postman who took the trouble to talk to the people on his rounds, and who moved from a sense of curiosity and joy about the terrain in which he worked to actively recording that fascination – writing himself and wheedling the stories, the poems and the recollections out of his friends and his neighbours. These books are a glorious celebration of the postman's unquantifiably essential role in rural Ireland. Required reading for officialdom within *An Post*.

'This is the bible of Connemara we have here . . . Learaí Ó Fínneadha opens a door, he doesn't say much himself, but he lets the vision do the talking . . . '. (translated from M.F. Ó Conchúir's introduction to *Ó Bhaile Go Baile* (1993)) The poet and seanchaí grew up in Lochán Beag in the centre of the Cois Farraige gaeltacht. His father was a poet and his mother was a fund of folklore and local religious traditions. His interest in traditional poetry was further fostered at Scoil Shailearna. In 1955, he married Maureen McArthur and settled in Barna. He spent most of his life working the land and his great love of nature and the countryside is evident in his poetry. He wrote over two hundred pieces of composition between poetry and 'agallamh beirte'. He was a mine of local lore, local history, local traditions and local politics. Also published *'Sé an Saol an Máistir* (1998). 'The poet wielded his pen/and took his basket/a man of the land/a man of the poem.//He was not here, but/for a short time,/his candle is quenched now,/but his comfort is still here.//He left our hearts/full of respect./That's that!' (A tribute written in Irish and translated into English by his grandson, Niall Watters.)

Talking to Fintan O'Toole (*The Irish Times*) about the recent TV series, *Seven Ages*, Ó Mordha pointed out that all previous documentaries on the Irish State were 'triggered by the Troubles of the last 30 years. The State here was seen from the perspective of Northern Ireland. It seemed to me that we had never told our own story in our own terms, from the inside.' To tell that story, Ó Mordha decided 'to weave together the living and the dead'. Interviews with children, for example, illuminate the motives of dead participants in the founding of the State. Nothing is given the gloss of distance. 'Ó Mordha feeds the viewer with the dissonant memories and opposed viewpoints of people who were, in many cases, willing to kill and die for one or other vision of what the State should be.' (O'Toole) Trained as a producer with RTÉ. Won an Emmy for his documentary on Joyce, *Is There One Who Understands Me?* (1982). Made two widely acclaimed studies of Beckett, *Silence to Silence* (1984) and *As The Story Was Told* (1995). Now has his own company, Araby Productions. Other works include profiles of Ó Riada, Yeats, Wilde, Parnell and the sculptor, Seamus Murphy.

In the year of his death, Ó hEithir received the Butler Literary Award in recognition of his two novels, *Lig Sinn i gCathú* (which topped the best-seller lists in both languages for several weeks at the time of its publication in 1976) and *Sionnach ar Mo Dhuán* (1988). The latter was seen by *Dictionary of Irish Literature* to be the 'greater in ambition, more deeply layered, and more fully executed' of the two works. A nephew of Liam O'Flaherty, Ó hEithir was born on Inishmore. Attended University College, Galway, but left without taking a degree. Worked as an editor for the publishers Sáirséal agus Dill, the Irish magazine, *Comhar*, and the *Irish Press*. Was a popular columnist for many years for *Comhar*, the *Irish Times* and the *Sunday Press*. (Some of these pieces are collected in *Willie the Plain Pint agus an Pápa* (1977) and *An Chaint sa tSráidbhaile* (1991)). Widely respected reporter and presenter of *Féach*, the current affairs TV programme. Other works include *Over the Bar* (1984), *The Begrudger's Guide to Irish Politics* (1986), *An Nollaig Thiar* (1988) and *An Aran Reader* (co-edited with his son Ruairí, 1991).

'The real people in his poetry are either those he knew or persons from history with whom he has an affinity. This gives his work, especially his later poetry, a wide public resonance that is often lacking in the work of his contemporaries . . . There is always the impression in a poem by Ó Muirthile of something carved, wrought, worked, turned, honed, shaped. It has an edge that cuts through to the mind.' (*Dictionary of Irish Writers*) From Cork. Educated at University College, Cork, where he was taught by Seán Ó Tuama and Seán Ó Ríordáin. At college, he was involved with the broadsheet *Innti*, which subsequently became a journal. Received the Irish-American Cultural Institute Award in 1984. Wrote 'An Peann Coitianta' a column for *The Irish Times* (subsequently published as a book). Still writes for the same paper. He worked as a journalist with RTÉ from 1972 until 1990. Works include the collections *Tine Cnámh* (1984) and *Dialann Bóthair*, two plays, *Fear an Tae* and *Liodán na hAbhan* and a novel, *Ar Bhruach na Laoi* (1995), which won the Duais Chuimhneacháin Sheáin Uí Éogeartaigh. A new collection, *Walking Time agus Dánta Eile*, is due in 2000.

CATHAL Ó SÁNDAIR 1922–1996

The author who helped revive and shape the popularity of the Irish language was born in Somerset to an English father and Irish mother. Brought up in Ireland, he published his first book at sixteen. Throughout his career he produced hundreds of stories – he was renowned for the monthly output of his latest Réics Carló detective novel – and once wrote a Sexton Blake adventure, *Bullets are Trumps*, using the pen name Desmond Reid. Adept not only at changing his name, but also his style ('even the great Réics Carló could not track down or solve the mystery of all my aliases!'), he wrote under various pseudonyms for *all* the main religious periodicals and national newspapers. When one publisher wanted his photograph included on the back of a new book, he obliged by returning a female relative's picture ('in keeping with Dad's veil of secrecy I'm not saying what this book is – but it is out there somewhere –' Tarloch Ó Sándair). His huge unpublished *Leabhar na Laethanta*, which took ten years to research, records in minute detail, in all Celtic languages, historical, political, religious and general dates in Ireland. It was donated to the National Library.

CATHAL Ó SEARCAIGH 1956–

Born in the Donegal Gaeltacht, Ó Searcaigh is an Irish-language poet. Studied French, Russian and Irish at NIHE, Limerick and Celtic Studies at Maynooth. Worked in Dublin as a producer for RTÉ. Recently returned to Donegal and lives on a hill farm at the foot of Mount Errigal. He presents his poetry at home and abroad and it has been translated into many languages, including Hindu. Works include *Miontragéide Cathrach* (1975), *Súile Shuibhne* (1983) and *An Bealach 'na Bhaile* (1991). *Homecoming* and *Out in The Open* are bilingual collections. His most recent publication, *Na Buachaillí Bána* (1996), is a collection of mainly gay love poems. Nuala Ní Dhomhnaill (*Watching the River Flow*) chose a poem about incest, 'Gort na gCnámh' ('The Field of Bones'), from that collection as one of her ten most significant poems for the final decade of the twentieth century. The furore that the poem caused is, as Ní Dhomhnaill pointed out, 'proof positive that poetry in Ireland is still taken with a seriousness that it has lost out on in most Western societies'. In 1997 Carol Moore made an award-winning film based on the same poems.

SEÁN Ó TUAMA 1926–

As professor of Irish at University College, Cork, Ó Tuama had an enormous impact on the many Irish-language writers (such as Michael Davitt, Nuala Ní Dhomhnaill and Liam Ó Muirthile) whom he influenced as teacher, critic, and mentor. (He himself was influenced by Daniel Corkery.) His anthology *Nuabhéarsaíocht 1939-1949* (1950) was seminal in highlighting contemporary Irish poetry. But he is himself a highly-regarded poet and playwright. While '[h]e does indeed have the quickness of intelligence and the adeptness of allusion which make him a witty companion and an invaluable teacher . . . he has a *duchas* and a *duende* which deepen the register and make him a poet of real emotional veracity.' (Seamus Heaney, launching *Rogha Dánta/Death in the Land of Youth* (1997)) He has written three other collections of poetry, *Faoileán na Beatha* (1962), *Saol fó thoinn* (1978) and *An Bás i dTír na nÓg* (1988). His plays include *Gunna Cam agus Slabhra Óir* (1967), *Moloney agus Drámaí Eile* (1966) and *Ar Aghaidh Linn, a Longadáin: Extravaganza Cheithre Ghníomh* (1991). He and Thomas Kinsella co-edited *An Duanaire 1600–1900: Poems of the Dispossessed* (1981). In 1991 he and Louis de Paor published an anthology of twentieth century poetry in Irish, *Coiscéim na hAoise Seo*.

CONOR CRUISE O'BRIEN 1917–

Conor Cruise O'Brien was born in Dublin and educated at Trinity College, Dublin. Assistant secretary general of the Department of External Affairs (1960); representative of the secretary general of the UN in Katanga during the Congo crisis (1961). Resigned. *To Katanga and Back* describes the period. Vice-Chancellor of the University of Ghana (1962–65) and Professor of Humanities, New York University. Joined the Labour Party; elected TD in 1969. Strong critic of Irish republicanism, publishing *States of Ireland* in 1972. While Minister for Posts and Telegraphs he amended the Broadcasting Act, leading to the prohibition of Sinn Féin and the IRA from the airwaves. ('Fianna Fáil grumbled rather incoherently and offered no serious opposition to the Broadcasting Bill'. *Memoir*) Lost his seat (1977) but was elected to the Senate. Resigned to become editor-in-chief of *The Observer*. A strong individualist, he joined the United Kingdom Unionist Party (1996) to support non-sectarian unionism. Married to Máire Mhac an tSaoi. Other works include *The Siege* (1986) *The Great Melody* (1992) and *Memoir: My Life and Themes* (1999) dedicated to the memory of his daughter Kate, who as editorial director of Poolbeg Press had encouraged the project.

'One gets very confused, you know, by accusations. I was young, and I was frightened . . . If people tell you you've written dirt, even if you know you haven't, some of it stays with you. I wanted to go away very far.' (O'Brien to Julia Carlson, *Banned in Ireland*) Born in County Clare, O'Brien has been haunted, but not artistically inhibited, by the success of her first, brilliant (banned) trilogy, *The Country Girls*, *Girl with the Green Eyes*, *Girls in Their Married Bliss*, which outraged and entranced in equal measure. 'Had any other writer written Night (1972), a night-time monologue in which one woman revisits her past, it would have been hailed as a masterpiece. On the strength of that performance alone, O'Brien's literary reputation is assured and further endorsed by A Pagan Place (1970) and any number of short stories.' (Eileen Battersby, *The Irish Times*). Has lived outside Ireland for the last forty years. Her trilogy (*House of Splendid Isolation*, *Down by the River*, *Wild Decembers*) deals with contemporary Ireland, its political and social traumas. *Wild Decembers* 'allegorises the clash of the old negative retentiveness with a new liberal flexibility and progressiveness.' (Éilís Ní Dhuibhne, *The Irish Times*)

Born in Claremorris, County Mayo, he entered the priesthood in 1979. His education and training took place in St Patrick's College, Maynooth (where, for several years in a row he won the annual poetry competition run by Kenny's Bookshop in Maynooth) and Rome. After his ordination, he worked on Clare Island before becoming a curate in Skehana, County Galway. He has written a number of plays and has published pamphlets on such issues as El Salvador, while his sermons are renowned for their literary quality (he harbours a strong belief that the nineteenth century tradition of literary sermons should be resurrected – Des Kenny). He now serves in Kilmeena. He is chaplain to the Galway–Mayo Institute of Technology in Castlebar. He also edited *Tulips in the Prison Yard: Selected Poems of Daniel Berrigan, Selected and Introduced by Pat O'Brien* (1992) and *Erect Me a Monument of Broken Wings: Writings by and on Padraig Fallon* (1992). A new collection of poetry is due this year.

'The most important attribute needed for poetry is a sense of how odd it is to be a humanoid. If you don't wake up each morning on a foreign planet, you can forget poetry as a pastime. You may take all the writing courses you want, but the essential ingredient cannot be taught.' (Julie O'Callaghan, *The Irish Times*) Born and educated in US, but moved to Dublin when she was twenty. O'Callaghan's first poetry collection, *Edible Anecdotes and Other Poems*, was a London Poetry Book Society Recommendation in 1983. This was followed by *What's What* (1991). *No Can Do*, published earlier this year, was a London Poetry Book Society Choice. 'The new collection again confirms O'Callaghan's sharp ear for the subtleties of intonation and speech as spoken, and above all a forensic feel for language.' (Eileen Battersby, *The Irish Times*) Poetry collections for children include *Bright Lights Blaze Out* (1986), *Taking my Pen for a Walk* (1988) and *Two Barks* (1998). Many of her children's poems have been anthologised and appear in school textbooks in Ireland, England and Canada. She has been awarded Arts Council Bursaries on three occasions. She works as a librarian in Trinity College, Dublin.

One of the most successful of the younger Irish novelists. His recent novel, *The Salesman* (1998), has been translated into twelve languages and is being made into a film. (Róisín Ingle, *The Irish Times*) From Dublin, O'Connor (brother of singer, Sinéad O'Connor) went to University College, Dublin. Younger than Roddy Doyle, he writes from the point of view of a much more physically and socially mobile generation (he himself has travelled in Spain, Central America and the US). Has written for the *Sunday Tribune* and *Esquire*. His first novel, *Cowboys and Indians* (1991), was short-listed for the Whitbread Prize. *Desperadoes* followed (the setting – Nicaragua; the central characters – Irish) in 1994. Recipient of *Sunday Tribune* First Fiction and New Irish Writer of the Year Awards (1989), *Time Out* Writing Prize (1990) and a Macaulay Fellowship (1993). Other works include *The Secret World of the Irish Male* and *The Irish Male at Home and Abroad*. Has written three plays, *Red Roses and Petrol*, *The Weeping of Angels* and *True Believers*. As an Irish playwright 'you have to write one set in a sitting room where devastating family secrets are revealed. I did that with *Red Roses* and *True Believers* is kind of a step up from that.' (to Róisín Ingle, *The Irish Times*) Recently published *Inishowen* (2000).

A person of diverse abilities. As a young man, excelled as an athlete. Irish champion pole-vaulter (1947), welterweight boxing British Universities champion (1950). Graduated from University College, Dublin. Attended Loyola University, New Orleans, as post-graduate. Called to the bar in 1951. *Oliver St. John Gogarty: A Poet and His Times* (1964) describes a man similarly awash with talent – surgeon, playwright, athlete, conversationalist. Wrote a biography of Brendan Behan, and performed a one-man show on the playwright in Britain, Europe and the United States. *Irish Tales and Sagas*, illustrated by Pauline Bewick, first appeared in 1981. *Troubles* combines personal interviews with leading figures and archival material to form a gripping account of a crucial decade. W.T. Cosgrave (first President of Executive Council of the Free State) described Michael Collins to him as 'the greatest Irishman who ever lived, greater than Brian Boru or Parnell.' Plays include *Execution* (broke attendance records at the Peacock, 1985) and *A Trinity of Two* (namely, Oscar Wilde and Edward Carson). Has written Japanese Noh plays and several volumes of poetry. Other works include *Celtic Dawn* (1984) and *Biographers and the Art of Biography* (1991).

'Bravely exploring grief and guilt, O'Donnell encapsulates heartbreak in a novel which is alternately terse and lyrical. Far from being a flight of fancy, *The Elysium Testament* is grounded on harsh psychological truth and is both horrifying and spell-binding. It shows throughout that the author is also a poet.' (*The Sunday Tribune*) One would say that O'Donnell is primarily a poet, were it not for the power of the two novels, *The Light-Makers* (1992) and *The Elysium Testament* (1999). Two of her three poetry collections, *Reading the Sunflowers* (1990) and *Unlegendary Heroes* (1998), were nominated for *Irish Times* Literature Awards. 'The poetry is striking for its combination of sensuality and convincingly intense emotion with an intellectual clarity. Her use of language is exceptionally deft, and her structures often perfect. She is one of the most imaginative and original of the younger Irish poets.' (Eilís Ní Dhuibhne, *Dictionary of Irish Literature*) A volume of selected poems is due this year. Scripted and presented programmes on writers Flannery O'Connor and Elias Canetti. Compiled and presented RTÉ Radio 1's weekly poetry programme, *The Darkness Echoing*, 1997–1998. Was drama critic for *The Sunday Tribune*. Currently consulting editor for the arts review *First Edition*.

The Donegal writer and socialist trained initially as a schoolteacher. Was school principal on Arranmore. Motivated by conditions endured by migrant workers (including those from his own district) in Scotland, he left teaching and became a union organiser. Fought on Republican side in Civil War. Was jailed for two years (during which he wrote part of his first novel). Edited *An tOglach* (1924–26) and *An Phoblacht* (1926-29). Led agitation against land annuities. Recruited for International Brigade during Spanish Civil War. Founded *The Bell* (1940). His six novels include *Islanders*, *On the Edge of the Stream* and *Big Windows*. 'At their worst,' says Bernard McKenna (*Modern Irish Writers*), 'they read like propaganda. At their best, they bring into conflict the forces and values of rural, precolonial Ireland and the colonial culture of the naturalistic, industrialised world. The latter strips the former of its virulence and forces the inhabitants to succumb to despair and poverty… The imaginative geography of O'Donnell's world vests in the ancient island communities of the Irish northwest the power to resist the oppressive forces of nature.' *The Gates Flew Open* (1932), *Salud! An Irishman in Spain* (1937) and *There Will Be Another Day* (1963) are autobiographical.

'We are always on a journey from darkness into light . . . Your birth was a first journey from darkness into light. All your life, your mind lives within the darkness of your body. Every thought that you have is a flint moment, a spark of light from your inner darkness.' (O'Donohue, *Anam Cara*) O'Donohue is a spiritual philosopher whose books, *Anam Cara: Spiritual Wisdom from the Celtic World* and *Eternal Echoes: Exploring our Hunger to Belong*, have appealed to a vast range of people looking for solace and spiritual renewal. He tells us that he was born in a limestone valley. That valley is in County Clare. He went on to do a PhD in philosophical theology at the University of Tübingen. Published a book on the philosophy of Hegel, *Person als Vermittlung* (1993) and is currently writing a book on the mysticism of Meister Eckhart, the early fourteenth century theologian, mystic and preacher, who was an influence on several later theologians and philosophers, including Hegel. He lectures and holds workshops in Europe and America, but lives in the west of Ireland. Has published a volume of poetry, *Echoes of Memory*, and has just completed a further volume.

Poets within the Irish Civil Service should be seen but not excessively heard. As Assistant Principal (and poet) O'Driscoll explained to Katie Donovan (*The Irish Times*), '[c]olleagues don't want the tone of the tea break lowered by talk of poetry. It is seen as an obsession on a par with golf.' But the world of work invigorates his poetry – business concepts, newly-coined phrases, daily life within the office all become usable material. Nothing is seen as unsuitably unpoetic. His sense of human frailty in the face of mortality was heightened and deepened by the early deaths of both his parents, but his first poetry collection, *Kist* (1982), while reflecting an obsession with mortality, drives its theme 'with an extraordinary, paradoxical energy.' (Bernard O'Donoghue, *Contemporary Poets*) He was a reviewer and a critic before he was a poet. '[A] maker of reputations at a remarkably early age (before he was 25).' (O'Donoghue) Much influenced by his close reading of Eastern European poets (with whom he was in sympathy from the start), his style is economic and ironic. Recently won a Lannan Award. *Weather Permitting* was published in 1999. '. . . this book is news, a real breakthrough.' (Patrick Crotty, *The Irish Times*)

'. . . although O'Flaherty's very finest stories were mostly written in the Twenties, it was in the Thirties that he produced *Famine*. This work towers over his other novels . . . possibly as close as the decade came to producing a genuinely great novel . . .'. (Brian Fallon, *An Age of Innocence*) O'Flaherty's life and background were fascinating. Born at Gort na gCapall, Inishmore, on the Aran Islands, he grew up bilingually. His father had a fifteen-acre farm. His mother's family, Plymouth Brethren from County Antrim, had come to the island to build lighthouses. It was intended that he should become a priest, but he lost his vocation and in 1915 joined the Irish Guards and underwent the trauma of the Somme. In 1917 he was shell-shocked and discharged. Fought on the Republican side during the Civil War. His first short story was published in *The New Leader*, a socialist weekly. *The Informer* (1925), a brooding, potent study of human nature, was successfully filmed by John Ford in the 1930s. He wrote prolifically over three decades. Most critics are agreed that his short stories represent his finest work.

'In their little worlds in which children have their existence, there is nothing so finely perceived and so finely felt as injustice . . .' . It is with this quote from *Great Expectations* that O'Loughlin flags the theme of his first book for teenagers, *Is Anybody Listening*? This disturbing and compelling story of one girl's reaction to the global injustice meted out to children was short-listed for the Bisto Book of The Year 2000. A percentage of royalties from the book will be contributed to Mukti Ashram (House of Freedom) set up to help children 'freed from bonded labour to overcome the traumatic effects of their bondage'. O'Loughlin's other books have been for younger children. *The Gobán Saor* was short-listed for the 1997 Bisto Book of the Year Award. Other titles include *The Yucky Prince* and *Fionn and the Scots Giant*. He and his daughter Aislinn (also a (frighteningly young!) writer of teenage fiction) have recently collaborated on a book of poetry, *Worms Can't Fly*. O'Loughlin was brought up in Birmingham and studied economics, English and history at Birmingham Polytechnic. Now a full-time writer, he previously worked as a teacher, a merchant banker and a music journalist.

Talking to Katie O'Donovan (*The Irish Times*), Mary O'Malley spoke of the pain of feeling herself to be inarticulate in Irish, the language of her grandmothers. Separated from her own language, the poet has taken English and beaten it into a shape she can use. It is an English manipulated by the undertug of another language. She was born in Connemara and attended NUI, Galway. She spent eight years in Portugal, teaching English at the New University of Lisbon, returning to Galway in 1986. Her first poetry collection, *A Consideration of Silk*, was published by Salmon Press in 1990. This was followed by *Where the Rocks Float* (1993). Her third collection, *The Knife in the Wave*, includes a series of poems commissioned by RTÉ to commemorate sean-nós singer, Joe Heaney. She is currently completing her fourth collection (working title, *Asylum Road*). She reads and lectures extensively in Europe and the US, and has done quite a lot of broadcasting with RTÉ. She has been Writer-in-Residence in Derry's Verbal Arts Centre, and in Mayo as well as having a long unofficial association with Inismore. O'Malley has been involved with the Cúirt literature festival for many years and is on the board of *Poetry Ireland*.

O'Siadhail is a poet and linguist writing in both Irish and English. Graduated from Trinity College, Dublin and studied Scandinavian languages and folklore at the University of Oslo. Lectured at Trinity and was professor at the Dublin Institute for Advanced Studies. He is now a full-time writer. In 1982, he received an American-Irish Institute prize for his poetry and he was awarded the Marten Toonder Award for literature in 1998. He reads his work regularly in the US and in 1985 gave both the Vernam Hull lecture at Harvard and the Trumbull lecture at Yale. He has broadcast extensively on RTÉ, French and Norwegian radio. *The Naked Flame* and *Summerfest* were commissioned and set to music by RTÉ. In *Hail! Madam Jazz: New & Selected Poems* (which includes *The Middle Voice* and *The Chosen Garden*), poems from the Irish collections, *An Bhliain Bhisigh*, *Runga* and *Cumann*, are translated into English. The collection, *Our Double Time*, was published in 1998. Other publications include an Irish language course, *Learning Irish*, which adopts a conversational approach with helpful phonetic spelling. He is a former editor of *Poetry Ireland Review*.

Okri first came to international prominence with *The Famished Road* which won the Booker Prize in 1991. His first book of poetry, *An African Elegy*, appeared in the following year. Since then he has written several further novels – *Songs of Enchantment* (1993), *Astonishing the Gods* (1995), *Dangerous Love* (1996) and *Infinite Riches* (1998) – and another volume of poetry, *Mental Flight*. His theme is the need for Africans to re-form their own identities and he uses magic realism as one of his forms of communication. He is Nigerian and was educated at Urhobi College, Warri, Nigeria and the University of Essex in England. His first novel, *Flowers and Shadows*, was published in 1980. He has also written two volumes of short stories, *Incidents at the Shrine* (1986) and *Stars of the New Curfew* (1988) – 'his deadpan, child-like simplicity of tone, illuminated by flashes of magic realism, creates the perfect medium for the telling of terrible tales.' (Arminta Wallace, *The Irish Times*) Winner of numerous awards, including the *Paris Review* Aga Khan Prize for Fiction and Commonwealth Writers Prize for Africa. Other titles include *A Way of Being Free*, *The Landscapes Within* and *Birds of Heaven*.

Both a poet and one of Ireland's most important editors. He has edited and co-edited *The Honest Ulsterman* (described in *The Dictionary of Irish Writers* as possessing 'a slapdash liveliness unique in Irish literary periodicals') from its inception in 1969 to 1989. He has also edited a number of anthologies, including *A Rage for Order: Poetry of the Northern Ireland Troubles* (1992), *Poets from the North of Ireland* (1979) and the *Long Embrace: Twentieth-Century Irish Love Poems* (1987). He was born in Enniskillen, County Fermanagh and graduated from Queen's University, Belfast. He has taught English at the Royal Belfast Academical Institution since 1971. Won the Eric Gregory Award for poetry in 1974. His first collection, *A Store of Candles*, was published in 1977. *A Northern Spring* appeared in 1986. Both collections were Choices of the Poetry Book Society. In 1992 he received the Cultural Traditions Award in memory of John Hewitt, after his publication of *The Collected Poems of John Hewitt* in the previous year. *The Ghost Train* (1995), includes love poems, elegies for his father and a series of small, haunting poems to babies being born into the uncertainty of the situation in Northern Ireland.

One of Mexico's leading poets, writers and translators, Pacheco (who 'has consistently refused to glorify himself, dislikes giving interviews, and places the poem above its creator' – Jason Wilson, *Contemporary World Writers*) was born in Mexico City and graduated from the National Autonomous University of Mexico. Having criticised Paz for his Parisian surrealism in 1957, he later (1961) reversed his opinion, concluding that Paz's best poetry had resulted from the influence. First came to prominence himself in 1958 with a short story collection *La Sangre de Medusa*. Two volumes of poetry and the novel *Morirás lejos* (*You Will Die in a Distant Land*) were published in the 1960s. Raymond Leslie Williams, University of Colorado, sees *Morirás lejos* as showing signs of early postmodernism. *No me preguntes cómo pasa el tiempo* (*Don't Ask Me How the Time Goes* By), the poetry collection which cemented his fascination with the passing of time, was published in 1969. '(O)ne of the most distinctive voices in contemporary Latin American poetry, at odds with the more literal and obvious political poets, as well as those who still affirm the prestige and magic of art.' (Wilson) Has published extensively since then and has won numerous awards.

JAMES PLUNKETT 1920–

James Plunkett is a pseudonym for James Plunkett Kelly. He attended the Dublin College of Music. After working as branch secretary for the Workers Union of Ireland, 1946–55, he joined RTÉ as assistant head of drama. While he was a senior producer with RTÉ (1974–1985), he made programmes on John McCormack (*I Hear You Calling Me*) and Cyril Cusack (*One Man in His Time*). In *Strumpet City* (1969) he wrote a wonderfully vivid, wide-ranging story of the struggle between Dublin's working classes and their employers before the First World War. It was subsequently dramatised on television. *Farewell Companions* followed in 1977 and, in 1990, *Circus Animals*, which, looking back at a period closer to hand, examined the growing conflict between changing social mores and Catholic teaching in the 1950s. 'Plunkett is particularly good at revealing his characters' feelings and at presenting them in a plausible way. Even his priests and nuns possess a rounded humanity despite the fact that they are portrayed as basically unsympathetic characters.' (Trevor Royle, *Contemporary Novelists*) As well as novels, he has written a volume of short stories, *The Trusting and the Maimed* (1955), several radio plays and *The Risen People* which was produced in Dublin, London and NewYork.

RUTH RENDELL 1930–

Crime writer par excellence. Writes both as Ruth Rendell and as Barbara Vine. Probably best known for her original creation, Inspector Reginald Wexford, and his gloomily intelligent sidekick, the aptly-named Burden. They appear in her first book, *From Doon With Death* (1964). Since 1990, they have been etched in the public mind through the highly successful television adaptations of the many short stories and novels in which they have subsequently appeared. She also excels at the psychological novel/thriller, in which the endless permutations of psychological damage are explored as she digs into the complex motives which drive people to do evil. Born in London, she worked as a journalist for West Essex Newspapers before becoming a full-time writer. *A Demon in my View* won the Crime Writers' Association Gold Dagger (1976). As Barbara Vine, she won another Gold Dagger in 1987 for *A Fatal Inversion*. In 1991 she was awarded the Crime Writers' Association Cartier Diamond Dagger for outstanding contribution to the genre. Her books have been translated into more than twenty languages. Some of her novel titles are *A Judgement in Stone*, *The Killing Doll*, *Talking to Strange Men*, *The Keys to the Street* and *Thornapple*.

MARY ROBINSON 1944–

'I am of Ireland; come dance with me in Ireland'. In December 1990, Mary Robinson from County Mayo, first female President of Ireland, invited her compatriots to join her in creating her vision of a more confident, more embracing country. Her election was unexpected. She was nominated for the Presidency by the Labour Party (from which she had resigned in the wake of the Anglo-Irish Agreement). Her career to that point had been outstanding. Studied law at Trinity. A scholarship to Harvard Law School was seminal in her education. 'I had a law degree, but I hadn't really been encouraged to think. And Harvard was just waking up to the fact that there were inequalities of sex and race.' (quoted in *Mary Robinson: the Life and Times of an Irish Legend*, Michael O'Sullivan) Appointed Reid Professor of Law in Trinity College, Dublin at the age of twenty-five. Elected to the Seanad in the same year. Highly regarded as a constitutional lawyer in both the Irish and European courts (dealing with such areas as the decriminalisation of homosexuality and access to legal aid). There was therefore some surprise that she should run for a position as potentially confining as that of President. She, however, created out of the Presidency a symbol of transformation, and as that symbol she effected more movement and change than the accepted powers of the Presidency suggested possible. She resigned before her term was over (1997) to take up appointment as United Nations High Commissioner for Human Rights.

NICHOLAS ROBINSON 1946–

A solicitor, he is also a cartoonist, an architectural historian and author of several books. Co-founded, with Edward McParland, the Irish Architectural Archive (1976). Co-founded, with his wife Mary, the Irish Centre for European Law in 1988. His book, *Edmund Burke: A Life in Caricature* (1996) is, in his own words, 'not a conventional recounting of Edmund Burke's story, but a voyage into the murky waters of propaganda and prejudice in late eighteenth century London.' From Dublin, Robinson read law in Trinity College and served his apprenticeship with the Dublin solicitors, Matheson, Ormsby & Prentice. Other works include *Heritage at Risk* (1977, with McParland), *Vanishing Country Houses of Ireland* (1988, with the Knight of Glin and David Griffin) and *New Lease of Life: The Law Society's Building at Blackhall Place* (1990, with Seán O'Reilly).

At a gathering in Kenny's Gallery last summer to mark his retirement from map-making, Robinson ('the last of a dying breed, who manually produce their maps in manuscript form with pen and ink' – Prendergast, Irish Institution of Surveyors) said, referring to technological advances in cartography, 'I would hope that when all this still raw technology has been absorbed into skilled practice and tradition, the ethos of cartography will reassert itself.' Author, cartographer and Irish speaker, Robinson was born in Yorkshire. Studied mathematics at Cambridge. Moved to Aran Islands in 1972 to write and to make maps. Books include *Stones of Aran: Pilgrimage* and *Labyrinth*, *Setting Foot on the Shores of Connemara* and *The View From the Horizon*. A dedicated environmentalist, he organised the campaign to "Save the Roundstone Bog" from development as an airstrip. His company, Folding Landscapes, produced his final map – an updated version of his original Burren map. In the course of his work, he has performed an invaluable service in rescuing old Irish place-names. Won a European Conservation Award for his maps of the Burren, County Clare, the Aran Islands and Connemara.

Author, most notably, of *The Wexford Trilogy*, comprising *A Handful of Stars* (1988), *Poor Beast in the Rain* (1989) and *Belfry* (1991), Roche is primarily a playwright. But he is also an actor on stage, in film and on television. Produced and appeared in his own play *Amphibians* (staged in 1992 by the Royal Shakespeare in The Pit at the Barbican) in Wexford in 1998. 'Instead of focusing on a male/female dialogue to expose the themes of his plays, Roche favors a polemic between generations.' (Hunt Mahony, *Contemporary Irish Literature*) He has said that his fascination with his hometown of Wexford deepens with every play he writes. Wexford amateur drama has been enriched. In 1996, the Enniscorthy Theatre group won the Esso All-Ireland Amateur Drama award with *Poor Beast in the Rain*. Roche grew up in Wexford and has worked as barman, factory worker, upholsterer in a car factory and builders' labourer. Sang with the Roach Band for five years. A novel, *Tumbling Down*, was published in 1986 and in 1988 he was playwright-in-residence at The Bush Theatre, London. Has won numerous awards. Currently working on a book of short stories.

Ryan, who grew up in County Laois and graduated from Trinity College in 1975, has written two very well-received books. *Home from England*, published in 1995, looked wittily and sympathetically at the trauma of returning home and finding nowhere for the changed person in the changed place that home has become. 'A marvellous first novel about emigration, inner and outer'. (*Sunday Independent*) The wonderfully titled *Dismantling Mr Doyle* (1997) looked with equal sympathy at the plight of Mr Doyle whose own world is changing around him. '[T]here is an undeniable touch of genius in this recognisable world, where standing in front of the TV during 'The News' is perceived as an act of sabotage, and washing up can become an empowering reclamation of territory that has been under siege.' (*Magill Magazine*) That rare thing, a seriously comic novel. A third novel, *Seeds of Doubt*, is due to be published shortly. It spans the greater part of the twentieth century, and is presented as a triptych of stories which, while capable of standing independently, are interlinked. Ryan teaches English and History in a comprehensive school in Dublin.

'John Ryan ran the Bailey bar and restaurant, where his contributors were usually sure of getting drink on credit, or even of getting a loan (which was rarely paid back, incidentally).' (Brian Fallon, *An Age of Innocence*) Ryan was the founder editor of *Envoy*, a short-lived, but important, literary magazine which also covered the visual arts (1949–51). During the first half of the 1970s, he edited the *Dublin Magazine*. While secretary of the James Joyce Society of Ireland he edited *A Bash in the Tunnel: James Joyce by the Irish* (1970). Born in Dublin and educated at Clongowes Wood. He trained as an artist at the National College of Art. He exhibited his paintings regularly and was much in demand as a set designer. He wrote a memorable account of the Dublin war-time artistic and literary scene, *Remembering How We Stood: Bohemian Dublin at the Mid-century*, in which all the contributors to *Envoy* – Patrick Kavanagh, Flann O'Brien, Brendan Behan and others – are captured. He was a regular contributor to the RTÉ radio programme, *Sunday Miscellany*.

Local historian, promoter of the Irish language and journalist. Seoighe has spent a lifetime exploring Limerick's past, becoming steeped in the history, legends, language, literature and geography and sharing his findings with the people of Limerick through his books, his weekly column (written under the pseudonym Mangaire Súgach) with the *Limerick Leader* and his lectures throughout County Limerick. Has had a long connection with Conradh na Gaeilge, the Irish college in Carrigaholt and Glór na nGael. Member of the place-names commission and honorary curator of the DeValera Museum in Bruree. Was awarded an honorary doctorate from the National University of Ireland (1990) for his work as an historian and for his contribution to Gaelic culture. He began his writing career in early 1940s, while working for Limerick County Council and his weekly literary and historical column in the *Limerick Leader*, begun in 1944, is 'probably the longest-running, continuous column in Ireland.' (Norma Prendiville) His books include *Portrait of Limerick*, *The Irish Quotation Book* and, most recently, *From Bruree to Corcomohide*. Is currently writing his memoirs in Irish.

'My wife and I have done a unique thing – started a university course that we can teach from home.' (James Simmons, *The Irish Times*) The Poets' House in Falcarragh, County Donegal (it had an earlier existence in Islandmagee, County Antrim) was established in 1996. The centre offers an MA in Creative Writing (credited by Lancaster University) and runs summer workshops, seminars and poetry readings for visiting students. It is situated in the Donegal Gaeltacht, and has been assisted by a number of diverse bodies. The venture has provided an extra intellectual and artistic stimulus to an already vibrant area. Two graduates have won the Patrick Kavanagh Award. James Simmons is a poet who mixes the serious with the light in a way which dismays certain critics. 'However, most reviewers are able to distinguish his poetry from his songs and praise the accomplishment of both within each one's individual genre.' (Bernard McKenna, *Modern Irish Writers*). Edited the *Honest Ulsterman* for several years. Janice Fitzpatrick-Simmons is an Irish-American poet. She has lived in Ireland for twelve years and is the author of several collections of poetry. Both poets recently published new collections. *Starting at Purgatory* (Janice Fitzpatrick-Simmons), *The Company of Children* (James Simmons).

Poet and environmentalist, Snyder is described by James K. Robinson (*Contemporary Poets*) as 'a highly literate primitive (he calls himself 'archaic') who loves the world of the California Sierras, the American Indian, Zen Buddhism.' Won a Pulitzer Prize for *Turtle Island* (1975) and has won numerous other prizes. Born in San Francisco and raised on a farm outside Seattle. Educated at Reed College. After college, he worked at a variety of jobs, and his first two books of poetry, *Riprap* (1959) and *Myths and Texts* (1960), drew strongly on his experiences as logger and park ranger in north-western America. Eventually he returned to college, to study Asian languages at the University of California, Berkeley. Went to Japan to immerse himself in the teachings of Zen Buddhism. Returned to Berkeley to lecture in the English department (subsequently became professor). He is influenced by 'five-and-seven-character line Chinese poems . . . which work like sharp blows on the mind' (quoted in *The Norton Anthology of Poetry*). Other works include *The Back Country* (1967), *Regarding Wave* (1969) and *Axe Handles* (1982).

The life of the writer, Francis Stuart, spanned nearly a century. Born in Australia, he and his mother returned to Ireland a year later, after his father's untimely death. His first marriage, at eighteen, was to Iseult Gonne, daughter of Maud Gonne and Major John McBride. Fought on the Republican side during the civil war. A controversial figure, evaluation of whose literary achievement has always been overshadowed by evaluation of his actions during the Second World War. Eleven of his books were written before the outset of the war, which he spent in Germany. Was scriptwriter for Lord Haw Haw. 'It was exciting, it was terrifying. It was at the heart of history.' (Stuart describing the period to *The Irish Times* in 1996) Made broadcasts himself on Berlin radio. Sacked in 1944 for refusing to broadcast anti-Soviet comments. Was interned after the war. The autobiographical *Black List, Section H*, published in 1971, is widely regarded as his best work (the poet, Paul Durcan, has described it as one of the two greatest Irish novels of the century). In 1998, he was elected by Aosdána to Saoi, the organisation's highest position. The election divided fellow writers.

A woman whose spiritual well-being has been nurtured by the countryside in which she has lived throughout her life. She lives with her husband (the five children are now scattered, as is the way with children) in Inishannon, County Cork (where the family runs a supermarket and post-office) and writes prolifically. Her writing was recognised by Brandon, Steve McDonagh's Kerry-based publishing house, as being a lyrical portrayal of a mainly vanished world – a world where telecommunications was a switchboard and a pair of headphones, and a man's bicycle cost £4. *To School Through the Fields* proved to have an appeal much deeper than the mere lure of nostalgia and has been published widely. She has since written further memoirs, poetry and a collection of essays called *A Country Miscellany*. Her novel, *The Woman of the House*, was published in 1999 and its sequel, *Across the River*, was published earlier this year.

First the prequel (Jean Rhys's *Wide Sargasso Sea*), now the sequel (sort of). *Charlotte: the Final Journey of Jane Eyre*. 'I always knew that after about five chapters it was going to slip into this modern figure. Although I do enjoy trying to echo a voice, I wouldn't want to do a whole book in it.' (Thomas to Penelope Dening, *The Irish Times*). The book was an escape from the rigours of his biography of Solzhenitsyn, *Alexander Solzhenitsyn: A Century in his Life*. His subject is not pleased with the biography, which draws on interviews with Solzhenitsyn's first wife. (*Amazon.com*) Thomas sees himself primarily as a poet – 'his early work in this medium was notable for the way it ranged across the heights of the fantasy worlds of science fiction and the stocking-topped suspender-belt of sensuality.' (John Cotton, *Contemporary Novelists*) But best-known as author of *The White Hotel*, his third novel, in which an individual hysteria is 'paralleled by the perverted mass hysteria' (Cotton) of a world in which Jewish massacres can take place. Short-listed for the Booker Prize (1981), translated into twenty languages. Has written eleven novels since then, including the quintet collectively known as *Russian Nights*.

Tóibín established himself as a major fiction writer with his very first novel, *The South*, which won the *Irish Times*/Aer Lingus Award in 1991 and was short-listed for the Booker Prize. *The Heather Blazing* (1992) won the Encore Award for best second novel ('that scrupulous judge [the main character] has, at an emotional level, never progressed beyond the stilted child who has frozen his incommensurable grief to avoid being hurt by it.' – Dermot Bolger, *The Irish Times*) Tóibín's non-fiction *Walking along the Border* (with photographs by Tony O'Shea – republished as *Bad Blood*) and *Homage to Barcelona* established him as a perceptive traveller through place and mind and this reputation was solidified with *The Sign of the Cross: Travels in Catholic Europe* (1995). *The Story of the Night* (1996) was seen by many as his most ambitious novel. Set in Argentina, the protagonist comes to terms with his homosexuality as Argentina and Britain confront each other over the Falklands. His reputation has continued to grow with *The Blackwater Lightship* (1999), again shortlisted for the Booker Prize. Co-edited with Carmen Callil *The Modern Library: The 200 Best Novels in English since 1950* (1999). From County Wexford, Tóibín has worked as journalist, columnist and editor for various publications.

'An Irishman, sober, will say not what he thinks but what he believes you would like him to think; he is a man of honeyed words, anxious to flatter and soothe, cajole and caress. When he has taken a jar or two and is in the mood for trailing his coat, he will say whatever he judges will give the greatest offence. In neither case does he reveal his own true thoughts if, to be sure, he has any.' Englishwoman, Honor Tracy, introducing the best-known of her many entertainingly satiric books on Irish post-war life – *Mind you, I've said Nothing!* (1953) – ('made a brief stir in the early Fifties', Brian Fallon, *An Age of Innocence*). Worked for Ministry of Information as a Japanese specialist during war. Sent to Japan by *Observer* in 1947. *Kakemono* (1950) describes Japan during the American occupation. Wrote several books on Spain, most notably, *Notes on a Spanish Journey*. Spent many years in Ireland. 'Her characters . . . are so gorgeously ridiculous that it is hard to read any of her novels without chuckling out loud . . . but neither her characters nor their adventures are finally memorable.' (Mary Rose Callaghan, *Dictionary of Irish Writers*)

WILLIAM TREVOR 1928–

Born in Mitchelstown, County Cork. His father was a bank manager and the family was regularly moved from town to town during Trevor's childhood. Educated in Trinity College, Dublin. Before becoming a full-time writer he taught both history and art, wrote advertising copy and worked for a period as a sculptor. Has won numerous prizes for his work, including the Hawthornden prize, Heinemann, Whitbread and BAFTA awards. 'As the Northern crisis obtruded more and more on his consciousness, Trevor began to explore his own past, both in its traditional Anglo-Irish dimension . . . and in relation to the Northern Troubles, as well as the unadorned world of rural Ireland.' (Terence Killeen, *The Irish Times*) The novel, *Felicia's Journey*, was recently filmed. '[O]ptimism is always very qualified in Trevor's fiction and very hard-won.' (Jay L. Halio, *Contemporary Novelists*) Bridie, in *The Ballroom of Romance* (televised in 1982), maintains a measure of optimism by reducing her expectations to the newly possible with each downturn in her situation. *Death in Summer* (1998) examines, amongst other things, goodness, and a hopeless and obsessive search for love by one who has never experienced it. In 1999 he was awarded the David Cohen British Literature Prize for a lifetime's literary achievement.

ZDENEK URBÁNEK 1917–

In the Czech Republic, Urbánek is known as a critic, essayist and novelist (in particular for the novel, *Ztracená zemé/Lost Land*) and as the translator of Shakespeare, Joyce and Dreiser. A well-known intellectual dissident of pre-1989 Czechoslovakia, he is a confidant of Vaclav Havel and was one of the original signers of Charter 77. From 1991 to 1992 he was Rector of the Academy of Performing Arts in Prague. *On the Sky's Clayey Bottom*, a collection of stories and prose pieces, was published in 1992. Urbánek (an ironist in the Kafka mode) has said that each of the stories in the book describes 'the experience of a freely thinking mind inside a country which was, because of the general conditions of the world, compelled to accept a totalitarian regime.' Commenting on the book, Stanislaw Baranczak (*The New Republic*) said that 'If the crime prosecuted in this courtroom of a book is defined as "silence," the victims as well as the oppressors, the people as well as the authorities, human nature as well as totalitarianism, are charged with it and put on trial.' Urbánek believes in the continuing necessity for Czech writers to 'maintain independence from moral, aesthetic and political stereotypes.' (Jan Culik, at University of Glasgow)

ANDREI VOZNESENSKY 1933–

In the late 1950s and early 1960s there was such an explosion of interest in Soviet poetry that readings were held in sports stadiums. Voznesensky (the great-grandson of an Orthodox archbishop) was, along with figures like Yevtushenko, a star of such events. Unfortunately his fortunes suffered a reversal when the authorities clamped down on 'excessively experimental' writing in 1963 and he was denounced by Kruschev himself as a 'bourgeois formalist'. He wrote an 'ironic' recantation which was published in *Pravda*, but for the rest of that decade and much of the next he did not return to full favour. 'Akhillesogo serdtse' (My Achilles Heart) and 'Avtoportret' (Self-Portrait) describe his anguish during that period. The 'much anthologized and much performed 'Goya' exemplifies many features of Voznesenskii's poetry. Extensive alliteration and assonance dominate the poem to such an extent that its semantic meaning . . . is in danger of being submerged.' (Michael Pursglove, *Contemporary World Writers*) Despite such criticism, Voznesensky's mature voice, evident in *Rov* (The Ditch) 'one of the key documents of the Gorbachov era', has been recognised as 'confirming his position at the forefront of Russian literature'. (Pursglove) He trained originally as an architect. Pasternak became his mentor and his first volume of poetry, *Fire in the Architectural Institute*, was published in 1958.

DEREK WALCOTT 1930–

Reviewing *Tiepolo's Hound*, a 164-page poem in which the poet parallels his own life with that of Camille Pissarro, A. Alvarez (*The New York Review of Books*) says that '[b]oth of them were outsiders from the start – children with talent and ambition in indolent backwaters, internal exiles whether they left home or stayed put.' Walcott's poetry charts his conflicting senses of simultaneous attraction to and alienation from the different cultures to which he has some allegiance, whether it be the English literary tradition or native West Indian culture, whether by birth or by choice, but '[p]erhaps his most enduring theme is evil'. (*Norton Anthology of Poetry*) Born in St. Lucia. Graduated from the University of the West Indies. Has taught at Columbia, Yale and Harvard. Professor of English at Boston University. Won the Nobel Prize for Literature in 1992. Inherited a love of painting from his father (whom he knew only through his painting) and *Tiepolo's Hound* is illustrated with his watercolours, but (talking of his painting) – 'I just don't have that bursting confidence . . . It's all very Methodist' (quoted, *The New York Review*). He has also written extensively for the theatre.

In 1991, *The Irish Times* devoted its annual fiction series to the work of contemporary Irish women writers. Caroline Walsh, who edited *The Irish Times* fiction series throughout the 1980s, subsequently edited the anthology, *Virgins and Hyacinths*. In her introduction she said that '[t]he chief delight of reading manuscripts for a women's fiction series was watching how, gradually, the threads became interwoven as themes echoed one another in story after story, confirming each other, questioning one another; making a dialogue. Like the Aborigines' songlines, a pattern, a patchwork of coherence, was emerging and it had no beginning and no end.' In the week that she became Literary Editor of *The Irish Times*, the books pages increased from two to four. She was born in Dublin and brought up mainly in County Meath. She has been a journalist with *The Irish Times* for twenty-five years. She has edited several collections of Irish fiction, including *Modern Irish Stories* (1985). Also wrote *The Homes of Irish Writers* (a book which is still in print nearly twenty years after its publication). Daughter of Mary Lavin, and married to novelist James Ryan.

The artist, Kenneth Webb, was born in London and grew up in Gloucester on the Welsh border. He lectured in the Belfast College of Art for some years before moving to Ballywater in County Down, where he founded the Irish School of Landscape Painting in 1957 (which he now runs in conjunction with his daughter, Susan, also a well-known artist). In the 1970s, he found himself lured south by the constantly shifting landscapes of Connemara. A derelict cottage near Clifden (purchased originally as a summer retreat) was converted into a studio, and Webb began his ongoing exploration and interpretation of both his own wild garden (with its massed fuchsia, purple loosestrife, montbretia, heather, daisies and irises) and the surrounding delicate, threatened terrain, a wild and subtly-coloured bogscape. In recent years, 'the range of his interests has narrowed, so that his work had become increasingly focused on Connemara, to a small section of the bog in Ballinaboy.' (Tom Kenny) He exhibits regularly at Kenny's Art Gallery, the James Gallery in Dalkey, County Dublin and with WH Patterson, Mayfair, London. He was the subject of a retrospective exhibition at Kenny's Art Gallery in 1990.

'An American audience would immediately pick up on the Generation X sense of disinterest and detachment, a "whatever" world, informing many of the poems. However, coming from a poet living, writing, and publishing in Ireland, this essentially apolitical and somewhat ahistorical attitude is surprising, and ironically rejuvenating.' (Rand Brandes, Lenoir-Ryne College, reviewing Wheatley's first collection of poetry, *Thirst*) Published by Gallery Press, *Thirst* won the Rooney Prize in 1998. He has been described as one of the young New Formalists. From Dublin, he went to Trinity College, Dublin, where he was an editor of *Icarus*, Trinity's student literary magazine. In 1994, he won the Friends Provident National Poetry Competition. As a critic, he contributes to *The Times Literary Supplement* and *The Irish Times*. He is currently based in Hull and is co-editor of the literary journal, *Metre*. A new collection, *Misery Hill*, is due to be published by Gallery Press this year.

The following is a list of the most useful sources of material consulted in the process of compiling the biographical sketches accompanying the photographs.

BOOKS

Abrams, M.H., *The Norton Anthology of English Literature*, fifth edition, W.W. Norton & Company (1986).

Barry, Sebastian, *Plays*, (introduced by Fintan O'Toole), Methuen Drama (1997).

Berney, K.A. (ed.) *Contemporary Dramatists*, fifth edition, St. James Press (1993).

Boylan, Henry (ed.) *A Dictionary of Irish Biography*, third edition, Gill & Macmillan Ltd. (1998).

Brady, Anne & Cleeve, Brian, *A Biographical Dictionary of Irish Writers*, The Lilliput Press (1985).

Carlson, Julia (ed.) *Banned in Ireland: Censorship & the Irish Writer*, The University of Georgia Press (1990).

Chevalier, Tracy (ed.) *Contemporary Poets*, fifth edition, St. James Press (1991).

Chevalier, Tracy (ed.) *Contemporary World Writers*, second edition, St. James Press (1993).

Dawe, Gerald (ed.) *Faces in a Bookshop: Irish Literary Portraits*, Kennys Bookshop and Art Gallery (1990).

Deane, Seamus (ed.) *The Field Day Anthology Of Irish Writing*, Vol. III, Field Day Publications (1991).

Degenhardt, Gertrude, *Farewell to Connaught: 65 drypoint etchings of the Irish West Coast*, Edition GD (1989).

Delanty, Greg, Ní Dhomhnaill, Nuala (eds.) *'Jumping off Shadows': Selected Contemporary Irish Poets*, Cork University Press (1995).

Fallon, Brian, *An Age of Innocence: Irish Culture 1930-1960*, Gill & Macmillan Ltd. (1998).

Ferguson, M, Salter, M, Stallworthy, J (eds) *The Norton Anthology of Poetry*, fourth edition, W.W. Norton & Company (1996).

Fitzmaurice, Gabriel (ed.) *Irish Poetry Now: Other Voices*, Wolfhound Press (1993).

Gonzalez, Alexander G. (ed.) *Modern Irish Writers: A Bio-Critical Sourcebook*, Aldwych Press (1997).

Harrison, Tony, *Permanently Bard: Selected Poetry*, 1995, Bloodaxe Books (1995).

Henderson, Lesley (ed.) *Contemporary Novelists*, fifth edition, St. James Press (1991).

Hogan, Robert (ed.) *Dictionary of Irish Literature*, Aldwych Press (1996).

Ishibashi, Hiro, *Yeats and the Noh*, Dolmen Press (1966).

Kay, Ernest (ed.) *International Authors and Writers Who's Who*, thirteenth edition, International Biographical Centre (1993).

Kennelly, Brendan, *The Penguin Book of Irish Verse*, second edition, Penguin Books (1981).

Kinsella, Cormac (ed.) *Waterstone's Guide to Irish Books*, Waterstone's Booksellers Ltd. (1998).

Lavin, Mary, *Tales from Bective Bridge*, Town House (1996).

Mahony, Christina Hunt, *Contemporary Irish Literature: Transforming Tradition*, Macmillan Press Ltd. (1998).

Maltin, Leonard (ed.) *Leonard Maltin's 1997 Movie & Video Guide*, Signet Books (1996).

McCafferty, Nell, *The Best of Nell*, Attic Press (1984).

McDonagh, Martin, *Plays: 1 The Leenane Trilogy*, Methuen Publishing Ltd. (1999).

McRedmond, Louis (ed.) *Modern Irish Lives: Dictionary of 20th Century Biography*, Gill and Macmillan Ltd. (1998).

McBreen, Joan (ed.) *The White Page: An Bhileog Bhán: Twentieth-Century Irish Women Poets*, Salmon Publishing Ltd. (1999).

Molloy, M.J., *Selected Plays of M.J. Molloy* (chosen and introduced by Robert O'Driscoll), Colin Smythe/ The Catholic University of America Press (1998).

Municipal Gallery of Modern Art (Dublin) and Rosc, *The Irish Imagination, 1959-1971* (catalogue of an exhibition held at the Municipal Gallery of Modern Art, Dublin), Trinity College, Dublin (1971).

Noel Duffy and Theo Dorgan (eds.) *Watching the River Flow: A Century in Irish Poetry*, Poetry Ireland (1999).

O'Connell, J.W., Korff, A. (eds) *The Book of the Burren*, Tír Eolas (1991).

Ó hAodha, Micheál, *Siobhán: A Memoir of an Actress*, Brandon Book Publishers Ltd. (1994).

O'Toole, Fintan, *Tom Murphy: The Politics of Magic*, New Island Books/Nick Hern Books (1994).

The Whoseday Book, The Irish Hospice Foundation (1999).

Uí Nia, Gearóidín, *Eolaire Chló Iar-Chonnachta de Scríbhneoirí Gaeilge*, Cló Iar-Chonnachta (1998).

Vallely, Fintan (ed.) *Companion to Irish Traditional Music*, Cork University Press (1999).

Walsh, Caroline (ed.) *Virgins and Hyacinths*, Attic Press (1993).

Weekes, Ann Owens, *Unveiling Treasures, The Attic Guide to The Published Works of Irish Women Literary Writers*, Attic Press (1993).

Wilson, Rebecca, Somerville-Arjat, Gillean (eds.) *Sleeping With Monsters: Conversations with Scottish and Irish Women Poets*, Wolfhound Press (1990).

JOURNALS AND NEWSPAPERS

The Irish Times, both on-line and on micro-film, has been an invaluable source of information, particularly the many interviews undertaken by Eileen Battersby, Rosita Boland, Katie Donovan, Róisín Ingle, Mary O'Malley, Fintan O'Toole, Arminta Wallace.

The Southern Review Vol. 31, July 1995, Number 3, Louisiana State University.

Lysaght Seán, "Michael Hartnett: An Appreciation", *Poetry Ireland Review 64*.

The New York Review of Books.

WEBSITES

www.salmonpoetry.com/ Salmon Publishing.

http://homepage.eircom.net/~philipcasey/irishwriting.html Philip Casey's Irish Writing Pages.

www.bc.edu/ Boston College for information on Adele Dalsimer in Irish Studies Fall Newsletter (1999).

http://homepage.tinet.ie/~writing/index.html for information on Eilís Dillon.

http://www.britannica.com/ Encyclopaedia Britannica for information and links on Bella Akmadulina, Margaret Atwood, Frederick Forsyth, Allen Ginsberg, Miroslav Holub, P.D. James, Denise Levertov, David Malouf, Les Murray, Sidney

Nolan, Ben Okri, Jose Emilio Pacheco, Ruth Rendell, Gary Snyder, Andrei Voznesensky, Derek Walcott.
http://www.pbs.org/ for transcript of an interview between Richard Ford and Elizabeth Farnsworth on PBS Online Newshour.
www.arts.uwa.edu.au/LW/nolan.html Lawrence Wilson on work of Sidney Nolan/The University of Western Australia Art collection.
www.websteruniv.edu/~barrettb/berrigan.htm for information on Daniel Berrigan.
www.arts.gla.ac.uk/Slavonic/staff/Czech_literature.html "Czech Literature and the Reading Public", lecture given by Jan Culik at University of Glasgow Igor Hajek Memorial Conference, 1995.

Particular thanks are owed to the following people:
Marie Boran, the Hardiman Library, NUI, Galway, for information on Michel Déon and to all the library staff for their invaluable and friendly assistance in locating material and answering tedious questions on how to focus the micro-film, work the printer etc.
Áine O'Connell for the translation from Irish of information on Learaí Ó Fínneadha.
Learaí Ó Fínneadha's daughter, Marion Watters, for information on her father, and his grandson, Niall Watters, for a poem and its translation.
Louis de Paor for providing me with Seamus Heaney's comments at the launch of Seán Ó Tuama's *Rogha Dánta/Death in the Land of Youth*, for a very helpful discussion on Irish-language poetry and for taking the trouble to read, at very short notice, some of the entries on the Irish-language poets (and for catching the worst of my spelling errors in the process of so doing!).
Joe O'Halloran for directing me to "The Centenary of Galway College", M.D. O'Sullivan's centenary lecture which Joe prepared for publication in the *Journal of the Galway Archaeological and Historical Society*, Vol. 51:1999
Padraic de Bhaldraithe and Tarloch Ó Sandair for information on their respective fathers.
Martin Byrnes of *The Limerick Leader* for information on Mainchín Seoighe.
The Druid Theatre Company for help and access to its programme notes and press cuttings.
The Embassy of the Czech Republic for information on Zdenek Urbanek.
My husband Keith for reading through everything, for his enormous encouragement, his questions, his suggestions and for his sharp editorial eye.
Tom and Des Kenny for endless help and patience in tracking down evasive information – in particular, I must thank Tom for his eventual divulgence of Pascal L'Estrange's identity (for some time my pride had prevented me from admitting I could find nothing on the man – on the web, in reference books, through casual enquiry, and Tom's enjoyment of Pascal's continued capacity to cause trouble quickly overcame any sense of guilt he might have harboured for neglecting to tell me Pascal's history when he first handed over the list of names!).
Finally, and above all, I would like to thank the entire Kenny family for the very infectious warmth with which they have embraced all the writers and artists who have come within their sphere over the years. As someone commented to me – 'they make you feel like Seamus Heaney whoever you are'. Without their encouragement and enthusiasm, not only for the arts in general, but for each individual struggling to be a part of that artistic community, this book could not exist.

Gabrielle Warnock